Politicians and Economic Experts

Politicians and Economic Experts

The Limits of Technocracy

Anna Killick

First published in 2023 by Agenda Publishing

Agenda Publishing Limited
The Core
Bath Lane
Newcastle Helix
Newcastle upon Tyne
NE4 5TF
www.agendapub.com

ISBN 978-1-78821-564-0 (hardcover)
ISBN 978-1-78821-565-7 (paperback)

British Library Cataloguing-in-Publication Data
A catalogue record for this book is available from the British Library

Typeset by Newgen Publishing UK
Printed and bound in the UK by TJ Books

Contents

Preface and acknowledgements

The genesis of this book lies in a comparative research project to understand how politicians approach the making of economic policy. Although there is already a substantial body of evidence on the voter side, the economic thinking of politicians is curiously under-researched. So, we asked 99 politicians and advisers from five established democracies – France, Germany, Denmark, the UK and the United States – to talk to us. What are their economic goals, and how do they think they can achieve them? How far do they draw on economic expertise? The book is about the intense and challenging balancing act they describe having to perform, between trying to achieve their economic goals and trying to please voters. It is about how this struggle may be particularly hard when it comes to economic policy, compared with other policy areas such as social or foreign. It is about how it may be becoming even harder as we navigate the post-crash and pandemic economy combined with deepening economic pressures from climate change. However, it is also optimistic, attesting to the determination and *potential* of politicians to find a way through.

By way of introduction, particularly for readers who are not economists, in this Preface I introduce three core themes of the book – economists, the populist threat and expertise – by setting out how three of the politicians I interviewed talk about them. The three politicians, a German Christian Democrat, a French Socialist and a US Democrat, help define how the terms are used in the rest of the book.

The first interviewee, a German politician who lost his seat when his Christian Democratic party fell out of favour, is talking about his economic ideas. He is passionate about them and keen to get re-elected so that he can pursue pro-market economic goals, deregulating and cutting taxes. His economic ideas came from what he saw as he grew up: the struggles to reintegrate the East German economy and to modernize and decarbonize. But he also mentions many economists he has read along the way, from Adam Smith to a cluster of German ordoliberal thinkers. And, even though he never formally studied economics, he has the greatest respect for it. He gives the most comprehensive history of mainstream economic ideas and economists of all the politicians I interview in this book. I apologize if economist readers find his sense of the history of economics simplistic, but he reflects the general understanding of economics and reference points of many of the politicians interviewed.[1]

The German politician sees the British economists Adam Smith and David Ricardo as the great "classic" liberals, who launched the ideas that markets should be free, and people should specialize and trade. The philosopher Adam Smith wrote the seminal *The Wealth of Nations* in Glasgow in 1776 as Britain was beginning to industrialize. Smith said there seemed to be an "invisible hand" that regulated markets. He also looked at how employers produced, how they were beginning to divide up their workers in ever-expanding enterprises and how notions of profit were developing.

Smith and Ricardo are the fathers of a long line of economists who the German politician, and some of the others, describe as "neoclassical". From the later nineteenth century, the neoclassicals set the economics discipline on the scientific and mathematical foundations associated with mainstream economics to this day. The German politician accepts their approach of seeing "the economy" as a sphere separate from society and politics. People behave differently in the marketplace; they become more self-interested. Economic forces operate according to various laws: prices are determined where supply meets demand; there are "opportunity costs" to doing things; and people respond to "incentives". Economists abstract from reality to produce models because they help to show such phenomena more clearly. The German politician calls economists "scientists" and respects how far their technical insights provide useful knowledge.

The German politician is familiar with the various schools of thought within the neoclassical body of economic knowledge. For him, Ludwig von Mises and Friedrich Hayek, associated with the Austrian school of economists from the early twentieth century, developed crucial insights about free markets and prices. Many see their work as foundational for the later twentieth-century economists who came out of the Chicago school. Like many British politicians, the German politician has read Chicago economist Milton Friedman, whose monetarist theory about how the supply of money affects inflation was influential in the early 1980s. Friedman's opposition to government intervention to achieve goals such as full employment and his push to deregulate business

---

1. If you are not an economist and want to learn more, a good introductory history of economics is Niall Kishtainy's *Little History of Economics* (New Haven, CT: Yale University Press, 2017).

and finance endured, even after governments stopped following his monetarist policies. The German politician is also aware of the economists from around the same time who have often been associated with a political and economic shift to "neoliberalism": the "supply siders", such as Robert Lucas, who believed in measures such as cutting taxes and regulation in order to stimulate growth.

The contribution of John Maynard Keynes, active from the inter-war period onwards, inspires respect in the German politician. Keynes argued that, when governments are facing a recession, increased spending – for instance, to build hospitals or infrastructure – stimulates demand and growth. This in turn will mean more people employed and paying tax. The government can then safely reduce its borrowing and will have the tax receipts to pay off some of the debt. But the German politician says that, as a free marketeer, he is less convinced by Keynes than those on the left. Keynes encouraged governments to intervene too much, through interest rates or taxation, to keep to the goal of full employment.

Keynes's approach to debt troubles the German politician. The school of economists he follows most closely are German postwar "ordoliberals". These are the economists, such as Ludwig Erhard, who lived through the hyperinflation of the 1920s and watched how economic policies that did not have long-term stability at their core contributed to the rise of Nazism. Erhard rebuilt Germany after the Second World War with the dual policy of a "social market": free markets combined with social stability guaranteed by welfare. The ordoliberals believed governments should not get into debt because it is not a responsible policy. Debt leads to higher interest rates and/or inflation. A government that is profligate today will incur costs for citizens tomorrow, endangering social stability in the process.

The German politician does not respect economists who are outside the neoclassical canon of thought that the liberals, ordoliberals and moderate proponents of Keynesianism are all based on. "Outsider" economists are often lumped together with the label "heterodox" to distinguish them from the mainstream or orthodox (Lavoie 2006). They tend not to be taught in standard university economics courses. They do not see the economy as such a separate sphere, and often challenge the assumption that people are self-interested in the marketplace. They may use some abstraction and modelling and believe some economic "laws" exist, but they tend to be more rooted in the real world, recognizing that the structures in society and power relations make a difference. Of the heterodox economists, the one the German politician is most aware of, and hostile to, is Karl Marx. He lived through the dismantling of Communism. He saw what he describes as the terrible state that years of government planning had reduced industry to when he visited eastern European countries in the early 1990s. Although this German politician does not respect "heterodox" economists, other politicians in this book will mention feminist economists who pay attention to gender-based power relations, ecological economists who want to totally refigure how people look at natural resources, and behavioural economists, associated with Nobel laureate Richard Thaler, who combine economics with psychology to study how people behave in the real world.

The second interviewee is a French left-wing politician, fearful that voters will turn to right-wing "populist" parties. The *Britannica* definition of populism is that it is a "political program or movement that champions, or claims to champion, the common person, usually by favourable contrast with a real or perceived elite or establishment". Some scholars (Stanley 2008; Mudde & Kaltwasser 2017) have described populism as a *style* of doing politics, of simplifying economic issues and appealing direct to the people over the heads of the elites or establishment parties, that can take either a left-wing or a right-wing form. But the politicians in this book who raise the populist threat tend to focus on its right-wing manifestation. For example, the French left politician sees the populist threat as Marine Le Pen's right-wing and anti-immigrant Rassemblement National (RN), formerly known as the National Front. Some of her centre-right colleagues are also fearful of the right populist threat, believing that some in their party may be tempted to go in a more populist right direction, whereby they beef up authoritarian social policies but appeal to lower-income voters with a left or "nationalist" shift in economic policies. As well as the French politicians, some of the US politicians used the term "populism" to describe Donald Trump, who had just lost the 2020 presidential election in the United States when I interviewed them. Populism is not a dominant theme for all the politicians I interview. The British, Germans and Danish politicians talk about it less, which is in itself interesting. Denmark and Germany have what many define as right-wing populist parties – the Alternative für Deutschland (AfD) in Germany, the Danish People's Party (Dansk Folkeparti) – but these seem to be receding in electoral strength somewhat.

For the French politician concerned about the rise of far-right populism, the problem is that voters have been in despair about their economic state since the 2008 financial crisis. They do not trust politicians to improve it. Far-right populists attract them in part because they either do not mention economics or they advocate simplistic economic solutions, which no self-respecting centrist would propose because they are unworkable. It is tough for centrist politicians such as her who do want to talk about economic policy seriously, because it is hard for the voters to understand.

This brings us to our third theme, of expertise. As a Briton, I am indelibly marked by the famous dictum by Michael Gove, the then justice secretary, in the run-up to the United Kingdom's 2016 referendum on leaving the European Union, that "the people of this country have had enough of experts". Gove was referring to what voters thought about experts, but what do politicians think about them? Most scholars agree that experts have to fulfil three criteria (Bertsou & Caramani 2020: 94). First, they must have specialized knowledge in a subject area, based on formal training, perhaps to postgraduate level. Second, they have to be objective. This is perhaps less straightforward. However, a third criterion, that experts should be independent, is even less straightforward.

A US Democrat politician, himself educated to degree level in economics, is exercised about how expert most economists should be seen to be. On the one hand, he respects a "great" economist such as Keynes who produced theoretical insights. On the other hand, he is not sure how many economists today can really be described as objective. Neoclassical economists have tried to present themselves as objective, unified round a core set of beliefs, like physicists or medical experts. But he notes how, increasingly, they take public stances that seem to identify them with one political stance or another. For example, he tends to agree with economist Paul Krugman, but he sees him as less of an objective economist, more of a commentator.

And, even if experts do not offer a political view, how independent are they if they work for the state? State-employed experts such as civil servants can claim to be independent. But in most countries, in the pandemic when "official" public health experts such as the United States' Dr Anthony Fauci, adviser to the president, or the UK's Chris Whitty, chief medical officer, appeared in news briefings, they often also drew on the panels of "independent" experts who were advising them behind the scenes. In the UK, for instance, the Scientific Advisory Group for Emergencies (SAGE) panel was set up. Whitty was a member, but most of the other members were university-based. In the rest of the book, I register what politicians say about state-employed economic experts. I also register what they say about non-objective experts: those who work for political parties or partisan think tanks. But much of what the politicians see as epitomizing independent expertise comes from outside the state apparatus, typically in universities or non-partisan think tanks.

The Democrat politician asks me, "Let me know who they are reading in Europe. Find me some genuine economic experts who are going to solve some of today's problems." But, even then, he says he is not sure what role he thinks knowledgeable, objective and independent economic experts should play in politics.

***

We were a team, based in the Politics Department at University College London, and supported by a UKRI Future Leaders Fellowship [MR/S015280/1] to study "mental models in political economy". I am responsible for much of the research design and the English-language interviewing, as well as the analysis and interpretation of the interviews presented in this book. But, although I use the "I" throughout to reflect that, I want to acknowledge the huge help I received from the rest of the research team. First, Marie Schwarzkopf conducted interviews with the German politicians who wanted to conduct the interviews in German and translated them. She also helped me to analyse them. We then moved on to interview Danish politicians. A majority spoke in English, but Maya Lahav conducted the Danish-speaking ones, adding great rigour to the translation of key words and her own ethnographic observations. Madigan Ruch helped me to transcribe the US interviews and Emma Elkaim-Weil translated some of the French-language ones and conducted one herself. We found ourselves interviewing during the pandemic, and were therefore forced online. We often found ourselves in tricky technical circumstances, with flickering internet connections, having to be scrupulous in data protection, and so on. We were also asking quite general questions, some of which seemed strange to our interviewees, requiring a high degree of professionalism. Our project team leader, Lucy Barnes, conducted and translated French interviews. She has been a constant support and intellectual sounding board. She read and commented extensively on all the chapters, prompting me to be clearer, and in our joint conversations, helping to develop the lines of analysis. I am also grateful for all the intellectual guidance I have had from Deborah Mabbett at Birkbeck College and for the advice of Matthew Watson. At Agenda Publishing, Alison Howson has been exceptional to work with. I also thank my husband, who is not a political economist but has had to listen to me rehearse these arguments; and my children, who are experiencing a tougher economic world than I ever did.

Anna Killick

1

Do we need more economic experts?

> You know, we're a democratic system, not a technocratic system ...
> If voters want someone else they can vote for someone else. They're
> voting on values, they're voting on the politician's ability to commu-
> nicate potentially quite complex economic issues in a sensitive way,
> and that's very important. (Economist adviser to Democrat senator)

> With increasing frequency, governments are outsourcing political
> power to expert institutions to solve urgent, multidimensional prob-
> lems because they outperform ordinary democratic decision-making.
> (Anne Jeffrey, 2018)

At the time of writing world leaders have just left the COP26 UN-sponsored
climate change conference. The Conservative prime minister of the United
Kingdom, Boris Johnson, arrived with a team of advisers from Number 10
and his chancellor of the Exchequer, Rishi Sunak, who made a speech on the
economics of climate change on the conference's "Finance Day" (Sunak 2021).
Sunak says his vision is for the UK to become the world's first "net-zero" financial centre, leading the way in promoting "green bonds" and encouraging firms
to be more transparent about their environmental impact. Behind Sunak is a
big parliamentary majority without many checks and balances, which should
in theory give him and his party scope to articulate and achieve their economic
goals. But, despite the UK hosting COP26, Sunak has been accused by Labour
and Green Party opponents of undermining the economic drive to prevent
climate change by cutting taxes on short-haul flights, and by being lukewarm
on transitioning from economic dependence on fossil fuels.

We will never know whether, if Trump had won the 2020 election, he would
have flown to Glasgow for COP26, or how much he would have talked about

the economics of it while he was there. Although the United States has so far been the worst affected of the five countries in this study by climate change, it also starts from the lowest base of national-level measures to mitigate it. But the proportion of Republican Party politicians who argue that climate change is not happening, or that the policy approach should be nil, is declining. And the Democratic president, Joe Biden, arrived signalling action, with climate envoy John Kerry. Significantly, he also brought his secretary of the Treasury, Janet Yellen. In Congress the recent passage of the fiscal stimulus package shows that Biden may share a two-party system with the British, but he has less scope for action. The Democratic Party's majority in the House of Representatives is wafer thin and unreliable and the Senate is almost tied, leaving Biden and Yellen with little room for manoeuvre, whatever economic initiatives they might pledge at COP.

Olaf Scholz was German finance minister in the coalition headed by Angela Merkel as chancellor, and is hoping to replace her as chancellor when the coalition is formed following the win by his Social Democrat Party (Sozialdemokratische Partei Deutschlands: SPD) in the recent general election. Back home, his political situation will be complicated both by Länder governments, which control some economic policy at the local level, and by how smoothly the Greens (die Grünen) and Social Democrats can work with their more liberal economic coalition partners, the Free Democratic Party (Freie Demokratische Partei: FDP). For the German politicians, policy on transitioning from their heavy coal dependence while sustaining their manufacturing base has been under way for some time. It has preoccupied politicians representing car-making constituencies or worried about rising unemployment in the east. It combines with other German economic fears about whether they are falling behind on digitalization or how they should extend their vision of economics within the European Union.

The Danish finance minister, Nicolai Wammen, arrived with the prime minister, Mette Frederiksen. The Danes have recognized and responded to the threat from climate change for longer than almost any other country. Their companies lead the world on renewable energy, finance and production techniques. For a country of 5.8 million people, they had a remarkably high profile in the 2020 US presidential election, held up by Bernie Sanders, the left-leaning senator for Vermont, as the epitome of the economic vision that Americans should aim for: a welfare-based society that has also made money out of being the world leader on environmentalism. Just before he arrived at COP, Wammen announced that Danes would issue the world's first "green bonds" (Buttler 2021). Back home, Wammen has to set economic policies that will meet Denmark's ambitious CO_2 reduction targets. His party, the Social Democrats (Socialdemokraterne), has formed only a minority government, and he may be pressed to go even further by far-left and environmentalist politicians.

Emmanuel Macron, the French president, arrived from France with his finance minister, Bruno Le Maire. Back home, Le Maire has the might of "Bercy" behind him: the powerful Ministry of Economy and Finance. Le Maire has said he supports allocating tax revenues from fossil fuels to finance the transition to a greener economy. But Macron and Le Maire face political pressures from both right and left; at the time of COP26 the governing La République en Marche (LREM) party had lost its parliamentary majority when dissident deputies who thought the leadership were not being radical enough on climate change formed a breakaway Ecology, Democracy and Solidarity group.[1]

Why were all these finance ministers at a climate change conference in the first place? Although the focus of most citizens following the COP conference is on the climate itself, sea levels, forests and biodiversity, the *economic* aspects of the environment are becoming ever more prominent. The presence there of finance ministers is far higher in profile than at any previous COP. There is a growing realization that no country is going to solve this (or many other issues) without implicating the entire economy. It is not just that the finance ministers will be the ones who write the cheques but, rather, that the economic remit is so broad and complex that any major change has important economic repercussions – and politicians are very aware of this, as they have been in similar ways with the need for unprecedented action during the pandemic response. Therefore, the question that is increasingly at the forefront of concerned citizens' minds is: will Sunak, Wammen and the others be successful in developing an effective economics to deal with climate change?

So much depends on these finance ministers and the other politicians in their parties. The economic conditions are important. They face different economic pressures, from the London finance sector, German manufacturing, US fossil fuel industries. Who knows what trends – in inflation, supply chains or some as yet unforeseen financial crisis – could derail them? Their institutional settings are also important, such as the constraints inherent in the US two-party system, Germany's federalism, France's semi-presidential system or the structure of civil services.

However, a lot also rests on the politicians themselves, their qualities and skills, their perceptions of their role as politicians. They will have to negotiate

---

1. After the interviews with politicians for this book were completed, Macron was re-elected in the 2022 French presidential election, with a rise in the vote for the far-right populist Rassemblement National, as some interviewees had feared. The legislative elections saw a fall in support for LREM and a rise in both the far-right RN and a new left and ecological coalition.

with other ministers and members of their parties, choose which sectoral groups to listen to and assess how voters are thinking. As well as working out what is politically possible, they will have to work out what is desirable, what their goals should be and how to achieve them and, crucially, who to go to for advice on what will be effective.

This book is about politicians' roles in economic policy-making. Economic policy-making is different from any other. It affects people deeply, but is technical and complicated and, some argue, best taken out of the political domain as much as possible. The book takes the finance ministers, opposition spokespeople and other politicians who work on economic issues in their parties to ask them how they approach translating their economic goals into policies, whether on tax and spending or mitigating the effects of climate change. It tries to find the answer to the part of the question citizens ask that is not about the economic conditions and institutional factors, but about the qualities of their politicians. It is a crucial question partly because, surprisingly, we have neglected studying how politicians see their role in economic policy-making at the general level.[2] But it is also important because politicians as a class are under unprecedented attack, with citizen trust in them at an all-time low (Pew Research Center 2019). Many citizens and commentators following COP26 have already decided they will not succeed, simply because they are politicians. And, indeed, the closer politicians are to areas such as economics that are technical, the less they have faith in them.

The need for a new "technocracy"?

One reason some have given up on politicians is that they do not think they are capable of delivering the "responsible" policies that are necessary for solving economic problems. Democratic theorist Peter Mair (2014) defines "responsible" as acting for the long term and in the interests of all. The problem is that politicians also have to be "responsive" to voters in order to get re-elected. Politicians' need for a winning strategy means that they are tempted do what they think is popular rather than what might be in the best interests of the country. There is a constant tension between politicians' "responsiveness" to

---

2. Scholars have interviewed politicians in national studies of economic policy-making (Fenno 1966, 1973), and in comparative studies of individual policies (Kemmerling 2017). Others have studied politicians' public accounts (Mudge 2018). But there are no recent studies of a comparative nature that I know of that are based on interviewing politicians, from across the political parties, about their "economic ideas" in general.

voters and their "responsibility" to deliver effective policies in the interests of all that undermines representative democracy.

Politician responsiveness to voters might not be a problem if voters were well informed. But voters are notoriously ill informed; and this extends specifically to economic understanding. Economists have long monitored the phenomenon of what they see as voter "ignorance", and are not shy in calling it that in the baldest of terms. But other social science commentators, reluctant to use terms such as "ignorance", use milder terms that hint at the same phenomenon. For example, Andrew Anthony (2013) describes the growth in a "comprehension void", caused by voters finding the economic conditions since the 2008 financial crisis increasingly hard to make sense of. A lot of the commentary on the Brexit and Trump victories focused on how many of their supporters had fewer years in education, the assumption being that having fewer years in education was more likely to lead to a lack of economic understanding. In the case of the economics of climate change, there is an additional dimension beyond lack of economic understanding, which is voters' tendency to focus on short-term gains. Voters may resist the long-term policies needed to mitigate climate change because they do not want to pay for something that will be of benefit to future generations.

Those who believe that politicians are not capable of delivering responsible economic policies often turn to technocracy, pressing politicians to cede some of their powers to independent economic experts (Majone 1998; Radaelli 1999; Dunlop & Radaelli 2020; Moravcsik 2002). If we were to go down a technocratic path in these five established democracies, what form would it take? I define technocracy loosely, as most social scientists do, as a "tendency within democratic governance to give ever more influence in decision-making to those with scientific or technical expertise" (Machin & Smith 2014: 50; and, for an overview on defining, see Bertsou & Caramani 2020: intro., ch. 5). In some countries technocracy takes the shape of experts being appointed as ministers, catapulted in without previous party political stances or experience. This has happened in some southern European and South American countries, but is less possible in the five countries in this study.[3] In these five countries a technocratic path would manifest as politicians consulting experts more often or giving them powers to set, if perhaps not goals, certainly policies and instruments. We would expect to see more deference to experts in posts "independent" of government, running influential panels or agencies at arm's length from parliaments.

---

3. In the United States unelected economists can be appointed as ministers, but they tend to already have a partisan stance. Of the four European countries in this book, whose constitutions make appointing unelected experts less possible, it is easiest to catapult in unelected experts in France (see Bruère & Gaxie 2018).

Until recently calls for ceding power and influence to experts have come from the right, and took the form of greater politician dependence on market-conforming economists in the neoliberal decades. But, as the climate crisis deepens, calls for greater power for economic experts are coming increasingly from progressives. Some scholars already note the stealthy process whereby experts in institutions such as the World Bank, the International Monetary Fund (IMF) and European Union institutions are extending power in the pandemic-ridden economy (see White 2020; Steffek 2021; and, for a critical perspective, van 't Klooster 2021). They note that these economists are less market-conforming and more interventionist than in the past. The current "new technocracy" wave is being driven by some of those who want strong long-term economic policies to mitigate climate change.[4] Anne Jeffrey (2018: 412), for example, argues that greater reliance on experts rather than elected politicians will lead to "optimal solutions" in a range of policies including "environmental sustainability". The United Nations' Intergovernmental Panel on Climate Change (IPCC) includes economists; it has held politicians' feet to the fire by pushing for targets in temperature reduction. Jeffrey thinks giving the economists greater influence over politicians makes it more likely that they will achieve the targets. Politicians could deflect blame if the economic policies were unpopular with voters, claiming that they were "following expert advice" – as they did with public health experts during the pandemic.

But a common criticism of technocracy is that it is undemocratic. It may be an improvement in countries where the politicians are highly corrupt,[5] but it cannot be justified in established democracies such as France, Germany, Denmark, the UK and the United States. The new technocrats counter this criticism, saying that technocracy reinforces representative democracy rather than undermining it, because it acts as a legitimate corrective to politicians' tendency to over-respond to voters. Although the editors of a recent book on technocracy, Eri Bertsou and Daniele Caramani (2020), present a nuanced set of views on the subject, some of the contributors (such as Dunlop &

---

4. As long ago as the 1960s some environmentalists, such as Garrett Hardin (1968), wanted further expert control over government to achieve what they saw as necessary radical population control. More recently environmentalists James Lovelock (2009) and David Shearman and Joseph Smith (2007) have argued that time is running out for tackling climate change and that experts need to wrest power from politicians.

5. Governments in eastern and southern Europe and Latin America seem to increasingly catapult in experts to be ministers (Ilonszki & Laurentiu 2018; Semenova 2018). Often the perception is that the elected politicians have already failed, by being corrupt or not capable of decisive economic action.

Radaelli 2020) see technocracy as a corrective to democracy rather than as an enemy of it.

The need for politicians' perspectives on economic experts

The subject of this book is *economic* technocracy. I do not make broader claims about the appropriateness of technocracy in other policy fields, because, for the sake of depth, the interviews were focused on politicians' beliefs about the economic field alone. The new technocrats raise two questions about politicians relying more on experts in the economic domain. First, are politicians *likely* to agree to calls for them to give up more of their power to economic experts? Empirical research into how politicians view the role of economists, whether at the height of the neoliberal era or at present, is lacking.[6] We do not know enough about how politicians see the role of economists generally, or how positively they assess any economist influence that has so far taken place. Hirschman and Berman (2014) argue that a key question when analysing how much economists influence politicians is how much politicians respect economists' authority. We will not always be able to trust politicians' answers on how far they have respected or relied upon economists' advice in the past, because of the potential for them to downplay influence, or maybe not even be aware of how far they are being influenced. But their perspective will nevertheless tell us something about how they have seen economic expertise. The answers to these questions will give us some indication of how far they are likely to give up more power as the climate crisis deepens.

The second question the new technocrats raise is whether greater economic reliance on experts is *desirable*, given the risk that it could undermine representative democracy. Many worry that over-steering towards responsibility without being "responsive" to voters' demands could provoke a backlash against expertise, or even representative democracy itself. Some of the scholars arguing that there was a strong neoliberal economist influence in the decades from the 1980s claim that the "depoliticization" those economists advocated was damaging (Burnham 2001; Fawcett *et al.* 2017; Scott 2021).

---

6. Much of the assessment that economists increased their influence over politicians in the neoliberal era came from examining policy outputs, or, alternatively, from excellent research based on talking to economists (Fourcade 2009; Christensen 2017; Campbell & Pedersen 2014).

Politicians gave responsibility for aspects of economic policy to arm's-length agencies. They passed control over interest rates and inflation to independent central banks. They privatized energy companies and gave control to technocrats in agencies that ran them, so that energy ministers were no longer directly accountable for the policy in parliament. They took aspects of economic policy out of the political arena so they could no longer be contested. Depoliticization angered voters who had not won from globalization. In this account, the excessive economist influence helped fuel a rise both in distrust for experts and support for far-right populists, who argued that they could have positive effects on the economy, for example by "taking back control" or "making America great again".

It is important to ask what politicians at the heart of economic policy-making think about the responsibility of their economic goals, their responsiveness to voters and the relationship between the two. We may not have to accept everything they tell us, but they are practitioners with in-depth knowledge.

The politicians in this book

The way to find out how and what politicians think is by asking them. My approach is to talk to politicians privately and confidentially rather than studying their public speeches or autobiographies. Confidential interviews reveal more about how they think when they are not distracted by winning over voters or the esteem of posterity. I have talked to 99 politicians and advisers. I have focused on elected politicians who indicate that they are interested in economics in some way, either because they serve on an "economic" committee or have a portfolio responsibility, such as being an "economic" opposition spokesperson or minister. I have talked to politicians from all parties, including some who have never been in government. Such a wide-ranging approach means I can bring out any differences that ministerial experience seems to make to politicians, and include politicians in parties that are not in government now, but may be in the future. So, to take just five examples, my interviewees include a former chancellor of the exchequer from the United Kingdom, a leading current Green party economic spokesperson from the German Bundestag, a far-right economic liberal who raged against the left consensus in the Danish Folketing, one of the most influential centre-left politicians in the French Assemblée Nationale and a prominent member of the Trump administration's economic policy-making team. I tried to reach across all the parties in each country. In some cases I triangulated with politicians' advisers, some of whom are trained economists. I put fuller details about the interviewees in the appendix.

I chose Germany, France, Denmark, the UK and the United States because I wanted to focus on wealthy countries that have a broadly similar political structure of liberal democracy combined with relatively well-functioning economies and some autonomy over their economic policies. If I had included Greece, for example, I might have found that the European Union's treatment of its economy after the 2008 crisis threw too much of a confounding element into the mix. And the five I did choose span what many scholars, from Peter Hall and David Soskice onwards (see Hall & Soskice 2001), would describe as the "varieties of capitalism", with the UK and United States examples of liberal market economies, Denmark a classic Scandinavian high-welfare one, Germany's "coordinated" and France's somewhere in between. However, I want to stress from the outset that this is, in some respects, a descriptive account. My focus is on accurately describing and interpreting the views of politicians. I assess what they share and where they differ, and I do draw conclusions from that about representative democracy. I think that, given the lack of previous empirical studies in this area, this is an important first step. But this book does not do the work of explaining *why*, for instance, German politicians have a different attitude from their British counterparts. Such an endeavour would require a more detailed analysis of institutions and cultures.

Interviewing from spring 2020 until winter 2021, in and out of lockdown, meant it had to be done online. There are many negatives: no insights from coffee served, chats with office staff, the chance to talk for longer travelling around with them or making the kinds of bonds people do face to face. But the positives are that, as organizing and conducting 99 interviews is logistically difficult, in lockdown politicians were often more regimented, less likely to cancel at the last minute. And, as anyone who has spent a lot of the last year on Zoom will know, you get to be able to read a lot from the screen image. There were national differences in clothing and office backdrops. I can report that US politicians are more likely than any other to have a flag in the background, but also to be in a wood-panelled office in their own home, rather than in front of a functional whiteboard or filing cabinet. And, in lockdown, we were often scared, which is one way to break the ice. Politicians were sometimes stuck at home without a printer, as worried as anyone about panic buying, dying relatives, catching Covid-19, what would happen with Covid-19. In fact, despite exchanges at the beginning about Covid-19, it was surprising how, as politicians got into the interview, it receded as an issue, almost as if they welcomed the chance to take a broader perspective outside the immediate emergency. Strange as some may find it, it was life-affirming to spend 18 months of gruelling pandemic talking to people who are such skilled communicators, and in the rest of this book the politicians take centre stage.

Plan of the book

I start with two chapters that set out what politicians have in common. In Chapter 2, overall, do the politicians aspire to make responsible economic policy as Peter Mair (2014) defines it? What do politicians think about economists? Do they think they are expert? How useful have economists been to them in their economic policy-making so far and do they think greater economist input would result in more responsible economic policy? Answering these questions will help us to predict how likely it is that politicians will give up power to economic experts. Four findings emerge. The first is that politicians see themselves as having goals that are responsible, and these are quite moral economic visions that they are strongly committed to. Second, they are divided on whether economists should be seen as experts. Some politicians do respect the authority of economists, but they specify that the respect extends only to one school or group. Third, many politicians see economists as too impractical to be useful. If they pay attention to economists, they seek out those who have done applied studies that address a problem the politician needs an answer to. Fourth, politicians have found economists less useful since the 2008 financial crisis. In addition, whereas Mair focuses on "responsibility" as producing long-term policies in the interests of all, politicians see responsibility as also entailing being responsible for making decisions, and then being accountable for them. At key points, including in the midst of crises, they have had to make the final decisions, even if they consulted economic experts beforehand, and they describe how that process feels.

In Chapter 3 I explore the pressure voters put on politicians. How far do they water down their economic goals and policies to respond to voters' demands? They nearly all make the judgement of voters that they are narrowly self-interested. Their views on this issue are more similar than on any others I touch on in this book, regardless of both nationality and ideological stance. At first glance this judgement of voters as self-interested supports the technocrats' case. But politicians are less critical of voters than one might expect. For instance, Remainer Conservatives and anti-Trump Republicans, or Democrats, do not diagnose voters as supporting those policies out of ignorance. Voters are their customers, "the sea in which we swim". However, although they are reluctant to lambast voters for lacking understanding, they go on to discuss some specific challenges they have had explaining economic policies. I show how, rather than seeing responsiveness as technocrats do, as "giving in to voters' demands", politicians see responsiveness as a two-way dialogue. Like democracy theorist Jane Mansbridge (2003), they focus on explaining their actions to voters as well as listening to voters. There are signs that politicians want to engage more fully with voters than in the past, a theme that runs through the national chapters and that I pick up again in Chapter 9.

There are national and ideological variations that I explore in Part II. In Chapter 4 I consider the attitudes of left-wing politicians to economists.[7] These politicians are confident that their approach to economic policy, their emphasis on distributive justice, is becoming more popular. They see themselves as driving a divergence in economic ideas in the period since the 2008 financial crisis, after the convergence of ideas around market-conforming economics in the neoliberal decades. Keynes operates as a catch-all for centre-left ideas, and the far left shows perhaps a higher degree of attentiveness to economists, but to non-mainstream or "heterodox" economists only.

The significant national variations in how politicians see economic experts and their relationships with voters are set out in Chapters 5, 6 and 7. In Chapter 5 I consider the case of Denmark and Germany, two countries often categorized as "coordinated" economies with consensual political systems. For Denmark I focus on politicians from all parties to show how there is a broad consensus of economic ideas at the political level and how politicians show a high degree of attention to economists, but only if they are "home-grown". I also question whether the attentiveness amounts to respect or whether, instead, politicians have the upper hand in the relationship. For Germany, because the perspectives of the German left have been prominent in Chapter 4, I focus more on the German right and its attention to and respect for "home-grown" economists.

In Chapter 6 I go to France, which is a fascinating case that confounds some predictions from those, including French politicians themselves, who have often seen economists as less influential in France than the Anglosphere. In France there is a greater level of respect for the intellectual contribution of economics than in other countries. However, the French are also most likely to see economics as a soft science. Whereas politicians in other countries tend to believe that economists should aim for objectivity, and there should be some kind of unified core to their beliefs, French politicians embrace the pluralism of economics. However, French politicians are most challenged by how to respond to voters, because of the twin diagnoses of "immobilisme" (resistance to change) and a populist threat.

---

7. I do not have a dedicated chapter for a "centre" category. For US politicians, I include "centrist" Democrats in Chapter 4, on the left, and centrist Republicans in Chapter 7. When UK Liberal Democrats refer to Keynesianism, I include this in Chapter 4. I include the German FDP in Chapter 5, which deals with the German right, because its economic ideas are so "liberal" and pro-market. French "centrists", such as LREM, and Danish Liberal Party (Venstre) politicians are included in the more national chapters on Denmark (5) and France (6), which cover all the parties in those countries.

In Chapter 7 on the United States and the UK, again because I have considered the left in Chapter 2, I focus on the right in both countries. Many, such as Marion Fourcade (2009), have argued that economists are more influential in the Anglosphere than anywhere else. But I find the US and UK right to be the least respectful towards and attentive to economists of any group.

What about the economics of climate change? Politicians' attitudes to the economics of climate change spring from their attitudes to economics more generally. This becomes clear in Chapter 8, which considers what politicians say on whether and how to respond to climate change and which economists they respect on this issue.

In Part III I bring the arguments of the book together and advocate a future path for politicians. By this stage of the book two themes are dominant. Politicians' economic goals are divergent and the degree of respect that they have for economists, and which economists, is also divergent. This makes it unlikely that politicians will be able to agree on which economists to cede control to. Further, although the picture is somewhat mixed, on balance politicians think it would be undesirable to cede more control, from the perspective of democracy. They are uneasy about the effects on democracy of past ceding of control to economists, believing it did fuel the populist threat. When economic ideas are contested, as they are at present, it makes it even more important that they stay in the political arena. As technocracy is undesirable, their only option is to engage more rigorously with voters on economic issues. They should not downplay economic policy with voters. They need to become "educators" when they talk to voters about economic issues. Some who already do educate provide a blueprint for politicians who want to raise the standard of their economic communication with voters.

In summary, to varying degrees, the politicians are predisposed to reject the technocratic path, but, if they communicate more responsibly with voters on economic issues, educating them, they have the potential to put democracy on a more stable footing.

PART I

Politicians' respect for economists and voters

This book is based on interviews with 85 elected politicians from across the political spectrum, with some under-representation on the part of some far-right parties, who resisted being interviewed. The politicians either have economic front-bench responsibilities, whether in government or opposition, or economic committee membership, so are predisposed to be interested in economic issues. In addition, I interviewed 14 partisan economic advisers or economists attached to committees. I chose to interview some advisers to triangulate what politicians said, but my main aim was to ascertain the politician perspective. As the interviews are confidential, throughout the book I give brief details of who is being quoted, such as "German CDU/CSU[1] politician", or "former British Conservative minister".

At the research design and interviewing stage I kept an open mind about how far politicians might share attitudes to economists and voters and how far they might diverge, and, if so, whether in national or ideological directions. By the end of the study I was struck by how much elected politicians had in common, more than might have been expected. Therefore, Part I of the book starts with what most of the politicians seemed to share.

In Chapter 1 I set out why it is important to research politicians' perspectives on economic policy-making given that many commentators, increasingly including progressive ones, do not believe that politicians can solve the complex economic problems we face and call for a "new technocracy". In Chapter 2 my focus is on what politicians share in their attitudes to economists. In Chapter 3 I turn to the second area where politicians share a common approach: their attitudes to voters and the economy.

---

1. The CDU/CSU is a centre-right coalition of two parties: the Christian Democrats (Christlich Demokratische Union Deutschlands) and, in Bavaria, the Christian Social Union (Christlich-Soziale Union in Bayern).

2

Politicians' respect for economists

A guy like Bruno Le Maire, who is the minister for the economy. He is at the top of a pyramid with ... lots of people who have a great training, great intelligence. Eventually, all the same, it is him [*sic*] who makes the decision, and he has to integrate all that, and he'll be tying himself in knots. There is little chance of making a good decision. You have to just look beyond the theory. You have to just look at what the global, big-picture consequences of a decision will be, and on what timescale, and, uh, at what cost. And, basically, that's it. It's not just maths ... it's also a bit of common sense and a quite deep understanding of the phenomena themselves.   (French centre-right politician)

Technocrats argue that politicians ought to listen more to experts, because, in today's complex world, experts are necessary to help them deliver economic policies that can be defined as "responsible"; in the long-term interests of all. But how likely is it that politicians will agree to listen more to economic experts? A crucial consideration is how far they respect the authority of economists. I start by showing how politicians think about the starting point for their economic policies, their economic goals. At this goal level, economists do not seem to have influenced them very much. But politicians may feel the need for expert advice when they come to think about how to fulfil those goals. Here we need to explore whether they see economists as experts. I take the criteria for judging expertise: of technical knowledge, objectivity and independence. First, how far do politicians agree that economists are objective and independent? Second, I take the other criterion of expertise: technical knowledge. Do politicians find economists' technical knowledge useful? This helps to build a picture both of how far politicians respect the authority of economists (Hirschman & Berman 2014) and of how far they have seen economists as driving economic policy up until now.

The "morality" of politicians' economic goals

Most supporters of technocracy accept that politicians should continue to set economic goals, competing with other politicians with different goals. The politicians agree; at no point in any of the interviews do they propose that it might be legitimate for experts to set goals. They talk about their goals in committed ways, as bedrock values and beliefs that drove them into politics. They may be more committed than most politicians; they had already shown an interest in economic issues as spokespeople and been prepared to give up time talking to us, but their commitment to their economic goals is nonetheless striking. A British Conservative says politicians must "be very clear about what things matter to you to achieve". A German Social Democrat says that "I want to do my part", in her case to achieve a "fairer society". They often say they developed their goals from an early age – late teens, early twenties. Even if they had formal economic education at that time, it is their everyday experiences they see as being most formative in the development of their goals. For instance, many recount observing a parent managing a business or neighbours who were poor.

Politicians are more moralistic in talking about their economic goals than one might expect. Although left politicians are moved by the desire for distributive justice, a topic I expand on in Chapter 4, it is perhaps more surprising how moral or normative right-wingers are in talking about what they aim for economically. Some right-wing politicians argue that they aim for growth and see its benefits as obvious, because people want material things. These politicians say it is not necessary to stipulate how the benefits of growth should be distributed. A French centre right politician says he is convinced that entrepreneurial freedom and free-market competition constitute "the best [economic] model", implying in his later comments that it is best because it is the most efficient one. He also warns that "you can't build a social paradise in an economic graveyard". To achieve what he wants socially, he says he first has to "do the economic". Right-wing politicians who are not obviously moralistic about their economic goals are more likely to refer to the economy as an autonomous sphere and the possibility that one might have to adhere to its "rules". A former AfD politician who was a trained economist says that politics fails when it "ignores the fundamental rules and laws of the economy".

However, many others on the right describe their economic goals as having a moral component. Some, usually in countries with strong Christian Democrat traditions, speak about holding "economic values" that relate to the need to help the poor by having a social market of welfare alongside a free market. One German CDU politician has always fought against socialism but has never been in favour of "freedom of the fittest"; economic freedom has to be accompanied by "responsibility, a socially bound market economy".

An American Republican with German ancestry talks about growing up with "values of thrift". He sees thrift as a moral value because it does not incur costs on future generations. A German CDU politician has the "goal of an appropriate distribution of income and wealth", which the market economy does not automatically achieve, so "therefore politics has to intervene". A member of the Danish Conservative People's Party (Konservative Folkeparti) says the values he has are more in the political and social sphere and he himself is a Conservative rather than an "economic liberal" in the sense that he values certain traditions such as environmental sustainability, family and community. He sees the economy as autonomous, but economic policy is "an instrument" for achieving these social values. Others in this normative group talk more about becoming aware, usually through small family businesses, that there was too much red tape, or that there was a value in working hard and independently of the state, which made them predisposed towards entrepreneurialism or free markets and that this is in itself a "value" that goes beyond their efficiency. An American Republican thinks he has economic values rather than ideas because "economic values are deeply embedded in what our view is of, you know, the individual and the individual's relationship with the state, so there's an underlying philosophy that drives so much of this. And so the economic questions, being value-based questions – it's sort of a deeper magic of human dignity."

Returning to politicians from across the whole spectrum, only a handful, mainly self-described economic liberals, see economists as having influenced their economic goals in these formative periods of political socialization. Most say the political predisposition – to have a left-leaning tendency to think distributive justice was important, or a right-leaning tendency to prioritize economic efficiency – came first, and then affected which economists, if any, they were drawn to. Therefore, in establishing how far they respect economists' authority, we need to look not so much at the goals themselves as at where they think economists are helpful in guiding them towards approaches to policy, the achievement of the goals.

One-quarter of politicians paying scant attention to economists

Before exploring economist influence at that level in greater detail, one group of politicians seems to pay almost no attention to economists at all, whether in influencing their goals or their approaches to policy. I invited politicians to interviews about "*politicians'* economic ideas". I asked one direct question about how "useful" they found economists. The other questions were about their own economic goals and policies more generally (as well as their attitudes to voters). This indirect approach means that I got a sense, in hour-long interviews, about how far economists are to the forefront of their minds and therefore how attentive they are to them.

Most of what follows is based on qualitative analysis of the interviews. However, I did also count references either to names, such as "Keynes" or "Keynesian", or to schools, such as "economic liberal", which, with some caution, also provide insights.[1] Excluding the unelected adviser interviewees, the 85 elected politicians made 600 references altogether, with about two-thirds of the references being positive and one-third negative or neutral. But seven elected politicians made no mention at all of named economists, whether negative or positive, and a further 15 made only one or two mentions. Therefore, about one-quarter of the politicians did not have economists at the forefront of their minds.

The inattentive politicians spent an entire hour talking about their economic beliefs based on their own observations and convictions about equality or the free market, reliant on political skill and intuition rather than reliance on the expert body of thought of economics. When pressed, with the direct question "How useful do you find economists?", they might refer to taking advice from civil servants if they enter government, or "economists", but without any elaboration. Some of the economists they say they read would be classified as journalists. They sometimes say that they read original sources of data and "applied" research, which helps them solve a particular problem, but that does not make them think of a named economist or specific school of thought. Most politicians still come from professional politics or lawyer backgrounds (Bonica 2020; Butler, Campbell & Hudson 2021). But the proportion of those with economics degrees among my interviewees, because they have all opted for an "economic role", is higher than for the average politician, at over one-third. It is therefore even more surprising that, in a group of politicians in which over one-third have received a formal economics education, as many as one-quarter are so inattentive.

Respect for economic experts: perceptions of objectivity

Of the three-quarters of the politicians who do talk about economists in the interviews, do they recognize economists as meeting the criterion of expertise

---

1. I define "schools of thought" very loosely, effectively as groups of economists or ways of thinking originally centred on groups of economists. This reflects how politicians talk about them. Key examples of schools they mention that would be widely recognized as such are "liberal", "Keynesian", "Austrian", "ordoliberal". But I also included vaguer references to "free-market economists" and other looser terms.

of "objectivity" (see Sánchez-Cuenca 2020 for a critique)? Most mainstream economists, such as those who subscribe to the neoclassical synthesis, aim to be scientists who strive for objectivity and a neutral stance (Lazear 2000: 100). Their claim to objectivity is based on a scientific core to their beliefs that they can all agree on. Fourcade, in her interviews with economists, finds them valuing objectivity and working studiously to "distance themselves" from politics (Fourcade 2018: 5). I show in this section that politicians' opinions are split on this issue. Of those three-quarters of the 85 politicians who can be classed as paying attention to economists, just under a half believe that there is some meaningful sense in which economists can be seen as objective. Just over a half can be judged as sceptical about their objectivity.

Those politicians who think economists *do* fulfil the criterion of objectivity tend to be centre right more than left. They tend to be describing mainstream economists who are associated with the neoclassical synthesis rather than heterodox. They see the objectivity of economists as useful in helping them understand what the effects of interventions will be and, therefore, how to achieve their goals. A French centre-right politician describes economic ideas as "a description of a system". A British Conservative argues that economic theories should not imply any particular ideology, but simply explain what the effects of various interventions might be.

This group of politicians indicates that they accept economists as scientists, at least to some degree. Some politicians are keen to stress the "evidence" base that economists bring. A centrist Democrat in the United States who is herself an academic, although not an economist, says that because she is an academic she favours "bringing evidence to bear in making policy decisions". Many in this group claim that they rely on economists, but the majority of their fellow politicians do not, to the detriment of policy-making. A former AfD politician, for instance, complains that the problem with most politicians is that they do not listen enough to economist advice. One of the politicians who has served in government, from the French centre right, says he relied a lot on advice, and also tried to bring economists in from outside the administration. Another former minister, a Danish liberal, says she had to get a crash course from economists to educate her, although she found she had to get a variety in because they were so specialized within subject areas. A German CDU/CSU politician says politics has become more complex, in part because of globalization and supranational governance, and that politicians cannot make decisions without the advice of "scientists" and their "models".

An economist who served as a minister in the Trump administration has personal experience of different mindsets of economists and politicians and the contribution the former make. He says that what economists provide are "big frameworks" that balance things such as "adverse selection with moral hazard" and draw on "supply-side ideas" about productivity.

> Whether it's the big-picture models and frameworks that have come out of our great economic thinkers, or it's just the way that all of us in graduate programmes are trained to approach economic problems and are then part of the framing of the decision that's taken to the key policy-makers, all of that, I think, is an important part of the contribution that economists serving these roles bring.

This former minister found a clash with the lawyer training and mindset which is the background of so many politicians. In his opinion, lawyers approach things in a "dramatically different" way from economists. They write laws to assert "command and control", compared with economists, who try to consider incentives and equilibrium conditions. What economists bring to politics is to point out the often unintended consequences of "command and control". Seventy per cent of his job was to "stop the stupid stuff".

Of those who were from the left who indicated that they accepted the objectivity of economists in some broader sense, by not immediately stipulating a particular group or school they thought would be most useful or by making direct reference to a lack of objectivity, one German Green says her economics training might have affected how keen she was for better economic "theory" to underpin environmentalist policies. A German Die Linke (The Left) politician on an economic committee regularly invited "academic economists" in to discuss issues.

Turning to the more numerous second group, who are sceptical about economists' objectivity, I find they are slightly more likely to be on the left, but still include many centre-right politicians. Their reservations centre first on the question of how "scientific" economics is. A common theme, as one British Labour Party politician says, is that "economics is not like astrophysics. There is more than one answer." A German politician says that economics "lives from discourse; nothing is fixed and lives for all time", so therefore it is dangerous to say that "we have a scientific opinion ... and all other scientific opinions are irrelevant". These politicians acknowledge that inevitably economics is divided, so that, even if politicians wanted to, there is no consensus of economic advice they could follow more closely. Some (often French) politicians welcome the diversity of opinion, and I consider them in more detail in Chapter 6, but most think it undermines economists' usefulness overall.

Politicians from the United States are more likely than politicians from any other country to interpret a question with the word "economist" in it as referring to partisan economic advisers rather than economists who still try to keep an objective stance out of the political fray. This comes out in the reflections of an American Democrat, who explains that he considers high-profile economists such as Paul Krugman and Robert Reich to be "social policy commentators rather than economic theorists". Krugman and Reich share his worldview, but he does not consider them useful because "their conclusions are biased towards their ideology" in ways that great economists from the past, such as Keynes, had not been.

His fellow Democrat also demonstrates the partisan nature of politician perceptions of economists in the United States. Like his colleague, he says that now, in the most partisan times he has ever known, there is no such thing as "an" economist serving a committee. Instead, each party appoints those economists as advisers who will "adhere" to what the party thinks. In 2008 this politician needed to decide whether to vote for the government bank bailout and stimulus packages. He says many of his colleagues consulted only the party economic advisers or the academics who were aligned with their ideological position. But he made it his business to consult a range of what he calls "independent" economists in universities, asking along the lines of: "Professor, you're pretty smart; this is what I think; tell me where I'm wrong and educate me." He says, "These are people who have studied the economy, the world, the international economy for their entire lives, many of whom have been recognized." In his efforts to seek out some he did think were objective, he is unusual. The fact that the economists at the forefront of so many US politicians' minds are divided into camps – and even labelled by interviewees with the prefix "liberal" or "conservative", "Democrat" or "Republican", in some cases – indicates doubts about economists' objectivity overall. With that comes a lesser degree of respect. American politicians are more openly transactional than those from other countries. For instance, an adviser to Republicans says that "economists could lend great legitimacy to your case by sheer fact of being 'PhD economist', preventing opponents from getting a purchase on your arguments". A Republican politician echoes this view: "What I have found with economists is you tend to seek them out when they validate your worldview, and that becomes reinforcing and you kind of use it as a shield and argument." A second Republican adviser comments that "in the USA, generally speaking, there's a little bit of a disdain for experts". The European politicians imply that a substantial body of economists keep themselves above the political fray to a greater degree than the Americans. Nevertheless, overall, the dominant perception is that, whether for political reasons or not, economist are often divided, and certainly cannot be viewed in the same way as scientific experts, who will tend towards more of a consensus.

The usefulness of economic experts

Whether politicians think economists are objective does not tell us everything we need to know about whether they respect their authority. As well as objectivity, respect for economists' legitimacy is based on their highly specialized knowledge of one subject area. Economists' knowledge is technical in the sense that it is based on mathematics, which makes them appear distinct and more "scientific" than other social scientists. Sociologist Michael Reay (2012) argues that economic expertise has an overarching feature that he calls a "core frame", based on specialized language, abstraction and modelling. He believes that the highly technical nature of the core frame of thinking boosts the status of economics in the political world, a theme that economic sociologist Marion Fourcade (2009) has also explored in depth. However, I show here that quite a large majority of politicians do not seem to respect the specialized knowledge or technicality of economists. They criticize economists for being impractical in ways that undermine their usefulness to them, affirming the arguments of recent scholars such as Diane Coyle (2021).[2]

Although economically trained politicians are among those mentioning economists more, they do not necessarily say they find economists more useful. A French centre-right politician typifies the answers of most of those who have been economically trained when he says his economic training has not significantly affected his role as a politician, because "I'm an MP who has always been immersed, if I can say so, in economic reality. For me, the economy is not just what I learned in school, or later at university, grand theory and monetarist – all that; it's not only that. Of course, it is that, but it's also reality, the everyday knowledge that accompanies it." A British Conservative echoes him, also dismissing "grand theory": "Most people's experience is what should be driving economic policy, not grand economics, sophisticated theory."

Many, including some who respect economists' objectivity, complain about how "over-technical" they are. A US Democratic politician is an example of an American showing respect for the value of objective economic advice *and* appreciating its technicality even though, like many, he has not been trained in the subject. He starts off by saying that "economists are useful". He does not listen to every word, but certainly "their analysis, their expertise, their professionalism, their charts, their graphs, are all very important to policy-makers". Note that he is keen to specify the usefulness of "charts and graphs".

---

2. Coyle (2021) argues that economists need to pay more attention to politics – in essence, become political economists – because they cannot develop optimal policy in a vacuum without considering what is possible.

He says they indicate what is happening with supply and demand, which he describes as "complicated". Nevertheless, he thinks the economists lay out these complex issues "pretty clearly" to politicians "responsible for making the decision". However, his almost textbook example of how technocrats might want to see economists explaining technical information to politicians is rare. A fellow Republican provides a more typical response. He recounts economists advising his committee to adopt a policy, but not being able to explain it well enough: "Now, it could be that it was just a terribly complicated proposal. Or it could be that we were just thick, and we couldn't pick it up. Or it could be a little combination of those or they weren't very good at explaining it."

Many politicians argue that economists are too technical. A German Social Democrat politician says they write "theoretical treatises" that presuppose knowledge he has not got and overwhelm him with their length. Some argue economists could make more effort to make themselves comprehensible. A French Socialist politician says economists have a choice: to "sit in their room" or "be willing to contribute to change". But, in order to contribute to change by influencing politicians, they have to know what the politicians' starting point is, such as by making their language and arguments accessible, and understanding where they want to get to, not just attempting to present "twenty pages of theory". A German far-left politician, with some academic economic training, who is responsible for developing his party's economic policies, says: "I have to honestly say that I personally have the feeling that [economists] do not shape me much and that they give me little, for, as long as the economic theory does not turn into some form of economic policy, it remains very, very academic for me."

Relatedly, the reliance on abstract modelling and mathematics reduces some politicians' confidence that economists' findings will be relevant in real life. A German centre-right politician has this evocative criticism of abstraction: that economists leave "reality" out:

> Yes, I met [economists] many times in parliamentary hearings over the years in Berlin. And my criticism of these people is their stereo-typed approach. They try to turn reality into models. And that always means that you have to leave out cross-connections or variations. And they were also, in the talks with the MPs, often trying to explain their model and say, "So this is how the model works." Only what happened to the side of the model was not discussed.

A German centrist says that economics is "useful, better than nothing, but it's only a rough guideline". He would not want to build anything on economic theory because "there are too many other factors that have to be taken into account". A French Socialist and former minister states, "It's difficult to do experiments in economics, and we see sometimes the same decisions; the same decisions have completely different effects because it's not the same period, not the same place, or it's not the same sector of the economy." A French centre-right politician colleague studied economics but says it "serves no purpose anymore" because, on the one hand, it is too abstract and, on the other, people no longer believe in "paradigms", such as the Laffer curve. "[Economic theory] used to be a talking point but now nobody talks about it. Today, there's no reference to an economic theory anymore."

A British adviser who was a trained economist, but with a relatively low assessment of the value of economics within politics, explains why he thinks there may be this gulf in understanding. He says economists are constantly thinking about things such as incentives and trade-offs even though "it's not how normal people think". He says: "Economists ... tend to see a problem and people behave in a certain way, and they'll think there seems to be some rational reason why they're behaving like this, and, if we don't like what it is, let's change that set of incentives. That's a classic economist's 'micro'[3] view. That's not how most people see the world, including politicians." Therefore, economists have to make special efforts to communicate to non-specialists such as politicians.

A common perception from the politicians is that they have to "translate" what economists tell them. A German Social Democrat says that the task of the politician is to listen and translate theory into practice, or into "policy judgements". The academic centrist Democrat who says that economists are an important source of evidence qualifies this judgement when she adds: "Sometimes the science doesn't tell you enough, and you have to make a jump into policy." A French centrist politician sums up how she does want to pay attention to what economists say, but how the challenge is to translate the economists' thinking into practice: "[I am] listening, reading what the economists say, but at the end trying to bring a response with my own thinking that I can myself produce in practice." A British Liberal Democrat argues that the role of the politician is to make practical compromises, which tend to dilute the importance of academic ideas from people such as economists: "Academic economists are very important, but are they influential as far as politicians are concerned? No more than academics in any other field. One of the key things in politics was that there are no really original ideas, you know. Somebody once

---

3. Microeconomics is the study of how individuals make choices in response to changes in incentives, prices, resources and/or methods of production, in contrast to macroeconomics, which studies how the economy behaves overall.

said in politics there are no solutions, only trade-offs." By explicitly arguing that economists are no more important than other academics, he challenges the Fourcade thesis (2009) that economists have had a disproportionate influence compared with other disciplines.

A French centre-right politician is "disappointed by economics as a science". He thinks politicians need economists, but economists are not focused on the subjects politicians worry about: "Economists want to be just as independent of the events around them as the mathematicians or physicists are. And so they don't want to compromise themselves by giving advice directly to politicians."

Declining respect for economists

Therefore, in the range and depth of their criticisms of the way economists limit their usefulness to politicians, through excessive technicality or a more general impracticality, politicians do not show much respect for their authority, at least as currently constituted. Many of the interviewees who refer to economists say economists' usefulness has declined during their adult lifetimes. A French centre-right politician says that economists are often used to justify changes but "there are *no longer* any who precede the changes". A Eurosceptic British politician says economists had "big moments" with Keynes after the war, and then monetarists from the 1980s, but not much since then:

> I can't think of that many big moments in the last 30 years where you would say academic economics has produced something that's been, you know, positively transformative in the economics of the real world. I think they've kind of slipped down the pecking order of usefulness since then compared to, you know, medicine and physics, all sorts of real science that's produced amazing things.

Some exhibit impatience with how the only big names to talk about are so old, writing about conditions that are now out of date. A Danish far-right politician committed to economic liberalism is frustrated that people refer to economists such as Friedman, and even further back, as the "big economic guys". He is "a practical man"; he thinks that, if debate is based on older theories, we "will miss the issues that need to be dealt with in today's modern economy". An American Democrat, with some economics education, says he likes Keynes, who was "foundational", but British politicians mention him because "he's one of their own", and "you know we're talking hundreds of years have passed, so I think you kind of have to update it a little". He dismisses the main economist he hears right-wing politicians calling on, Arthur Laffer, "who's just goofy".

The right-wing politicians use him to justify tax cuts, but it's a "simplistic theory" that they use to manipulate people because their real aim is to reduce the size of government. He does not think we have "outstanding economists today" such as Keynes, who developed "seminal" theories. Instead, we have "commentators", a term that embraces Thomas Piketty.

For some, part of the problem is economists' increasing use of mathematical modelling. A German adviser, who promotes "free-market" ideas in a country in which he thinks many voters and politicians are hostile to them, believes the Austrian school, economists such as Hayek, "give a very clear idea on what helps and makes a state more efficient, work better, and economy work better" because they tell a "story". Mathematical modelling may also be a valid way of telling a story, but it does not grab people's attention so effectively.

But these explanations about general disenchantment, declining objectivity or mathematical modelling are often intertwined with explanations about how economists have failed to explain the conditions since the 2008 crisis. Why did growth stagnate, why have interest rates and inflation stayed so low for so long, why have governments been able to increase borrowing without provoking some kind of reaction, violating many of the rules economists have laid down in the past? A French centre-right politician says that nowadays "the economy is never an issue, and people don't believe in economic debate anymore". In the past "we saw economists, people listened to economists, like they listened to priest in the 1950s. Now nobody listens to priests anymore, obviously – and then, the economists; we don't listen to them too much anymore either. Because the miracles that they announced never arrived, you know?" The same French politician adds that, if you had asked French economists whether the government could have borrowed the amount it has in the pandemic, they would have said that "the system will explode". But, instead, the system keeps working: "Each time, you put a little more water in the glass, but then the glass is still not full, you see?" Many politicians even argue that it is challenging for them to talk about economic policy with each other, let alone voters, because of how uncertain the times are. A Danish Social Democrat (Socialdemokratiet) says the times are so uncertain that many politicians "are afraid to speak up and to share their ideas, because even doing that, if they're key decision-makers, might rock the boat in a manner they are quite frankly scared about". A British centrist politician reinforces this view. Economists have not been able to explain secular stagnation following 2008. Until 2008 "the economy worked almost like clockwork", growing at around 2 per cent a year; then people's trust in economists was shattered by the crisis itself, but it was compounded by the fact that the "standard economic model" did not predict the full employment with falling real wages and stagnant growth since the crisis. "So, in a way, economics has failed." An American Republican who opposes high government debt does not understand why some say that now inflation is less of a concern then it has been in the past. He has been told that "the rules that I was always operating under are somewhat antiquated". But we always seem to find a way to create bubbles, and he worries that the current low inflation and interest rates will be unsustainable, "that things have a way of catching up".

A German Green references "the Adam Tooze argument" that we do not have enough data to explain modern economic conditions. She is really "depressed" that the debates in 50 per cent of cases "are not going to the point … the economical heart". Gaps in information have arisen in the last 20 years. She loves the Keynes quote that "first, you have the ideas, and the ideas that can become action can become policy". She adds: "But, to get the interesting ideas or the ideas that matter, you must have access to the relevant information, and I have the impression that the relevant information [on which] to draw economic theory and political theory right now is missing." A French politician agrees that we also do not know enough about the global- and EU-level workings of the economy. A German centrist politician who would normally want to pay attention to economists thinks that behavioural economics has extended their capacity to understand real-world conditions but, even so, "forecasting" is difficult. "And nobody really is in a position to tell you what's going to happen." Therefore, economics, as a technocratic, scientific endeavour, is seen as somewhat discredited by what these politicians see as recent empirical and disciplinary failures.

A further point about declining influence since 2008 is illustrated by a French centrist, below the age of 50, who studied economics at both undergraduate and masters level. He describes a "classical" economics training until the "ideological shift" in economics "pushed by the events taking place between 2010 and 2020". During this period economics was being "restructured". "Starting from the 2008 crisis, and later with the sovereign debt crisis, we started questioning [economists] more and more. Then there was Covid, of course, but also big political changes like Trump's election, the choice of Brexit, the reversal against international trade that is a little bit everywhere in western Europe and in US, etc." He sees a quite fundamental change in the relationship between what he calls "the theoretical structures" in economics and "the conception of politics". It may be that after a "time lag", when civil servants and partisan economic advisers have learned any new thinking produced by economists, it then becomes visible enough to politicians that they start paying it attention. He thinks that Robert Mundell's work on monetary theory may be an example of new economic thinking beginning to get traction, but because it is in monetary policy to some extent beyond politicians' control, thanks to central bank independence, the process is less obvious. But, more generally, he thinks politicians are not turning towards new economic thinking so much as being more equivocal about applying economic thinking to problems. The crises he cites, of Brexit and Trump's victory, have made them cautious about liberal economic approaches that pursue economic goals without consideration for social and political responses.

Shouldering "responsibility"

Politicians raise questions about the nature of "responsibility", the kinds of pressures on Bruno Le Maire in the quotation at the head of this chapter. Although democratic theorists focus on responsibility as producing long-term policies in the interests of all, politicians see responsibility as also entailing being responsible for making decisions and then being held accountable for them. At key points, including in the midst of crises, they have had to make the final decisions, even if they have consulted economic experts beforehand, and they describe how that process feels. The politicians are unanimous in claiming that it is they rather than economists who "drive" policy.

The politicians' sense of shouldering responsibility comes out strongly in those who were close to decision-making in the 2008 financial crisis. Several politicians also argue that making the decision to boost the post-lockdown economy with "Keynesian"-style demand stimulus and borrowing has been more straightforward than decision-making during the 2008 financial crisis. In connection with 2008, politicians give the sense that they felt quite alone, and I illustrate how they rely on economists by focusing on two individuals at the eye of the storm – a British minister and an economically trained British adviser – before bringing in some of the other voices.

The economically trained adviser to British Labour ministers describes how the 2008 crisis came as a shock that economists had not anticipated; in fact, "most of them had denied it would ever happen". As banks fell around them, he said "none of us had any clue what was really going on. There wasn't a lot of academic thought telling you what you did in a situation like this." The politicians just had to make fast decisions about how far to prop the banks up. He says: "And, in retrospect, the rescues we did of the banks and that we pushed on some other countries were the right things to do, but we didn't know at the time. I remember the nervousness round 'We're going to announce this on Monday when the markets open; God alone knows what's going to happen – we're in uncharted territory." After the immediate crisis of preventing the banking collapse was over, and they turned to stimulating the economy, they felt they were falling back on something more solid in the shape of "Keynesian" thinking. There were some specialists in labour economists who they approached for ideas about what would inject stimulus "fast". At the macro level they went for the VAT cut, but there were interesting debates beforehand about whether that would be the most effective route. "Some economists" argued that some of the policies they introduced, such as a car scrappage scheme, were "gimmicky" and not what their models advised. But the adviser says that the economists did not understand as well as politicians how to boost public confidence with schemes such as car scrappage, which actually turned out to capture public imagination and act as a symbol of confidence in the economy.

The minister broadly supports the adviser's interpretations. He says there were plenty of people advising him, but he relied on "intuition", "instinct" and "common sense". Politicians' common sense is an advantage over the economist perspective because they understand the mood of their constituents and are better able to judge whether, for instance, a VAT cut will boost public confidence to spend again. "On that level, it's about using your intuition to work out what might happen." In contrast, the economist has to rely on past models. The minister says he was already aware that Keynes would have agreed that they needed to "put money into people's hands", but he does not think any politician "would sit down and read an economic tome before coming to a decision like that".

These themes are echoed by others, such as this German CDU/CSU politician, close to decision-making, who describes getting a briefing from ministers at the height of the crisis. "At the briefing that we held there, we didn't know what to do next. People believed that we at the centre of political power knew exactly what to do next. We didn't know. We only had guesses and had to make decisions based on the guesses." A recurrent theme for politicians is that, whether in this crisis or not, they often have to take decisions quickly. As this German politician says, "You often have to decide very quickly, even though you only know 60 to 70 per cent of the facts." This adds to the sense of responsibility. A US Midwesterner Republican politician calls decision-making in the 2008 crisis "scary" and a "pretty big burden". A Democrat felt the weight of responsibility keenly: "People were asking me to give trillions of dollars of taxpayer money right now – like, this very second – or we'll go into the next depression."

The most positive model put forward proactively by about one-fifth of the interviewees is that they make efforts to learn from economists, listening closely – a process we have already seen some describe. A German centre-right politician describes how, after listening, in his case to the Council of Economic Experts, he also has to be aware that a scientific council can be only what it is, "namely *scientifically* and not *politically* responsible. In the end, there have to be decisions that someone has to take, and for this they cannot rely solely on science – i.e. politics remains responsible." This is echoed by his centre-right colleague: "Politicians are not obliged to implement the advice of science, but they must know and listen to science. Afterwards, politicians alone can decide." An American Republican says the job of the politician is "to hear [economists'] point of view and then make a decision or a value judgement about the right policy or the direction to go".

We need to treat these claims that it is politicians, not economists, who shoulder responsibility with some caution, because elected politicians may have an inflated sense of their own importance. But the unanimity with which they make the claim is nevertheless striking. And, as I show in Chapter 9, they have some doubts about whether their past ceding of control, such as in the wave of reforms associated with depoliticizing economic policy in the neoliberal decades, had positive benefits.

Which economists are respected?

Although I have talked so far mainly about politicians' views of economists in general, many stipulate a particular group they follow or find useful. The quantitative analysis of numbers of politician mentions of economists I refer to at the start of the chapter gives some additional insights into *which* economists politicians mention.[4] Table 2.1 shows the ten most frequently cited. It shows positive mentions only. I set quite a high bar for "positive"; if they are ambivalent, I categorize them as "neutral".

Table 2.1 also illuminates this point about the decline in economists' influence in the recent past, because so few of the most-mentioned economists have written in the twenty-first century. Table 2.2 isolates economists writing in the twenty-first century and shows those who politicians make most

---

4. I have coded all positive references to economists and schools by politicians. I allow for latitude in interpreting what counts as an economist or school. For example, I include "liberal" if succeeded by "economic" or, alternatively, in the case of some Americans, "liberal economists", used to describe economists they perceived to be on the left. But I do not code references to "liberal" or "neoliberal" or "socialist" when the speaker is referring to a political rather than an economic position. In order to keep the focus on named economists and schools I exclude "free market" as a general descriptor unless followed by "economist". I include mentions of named economists or economic schools of thought, but also generic references to types of economists serving in institutions such as the US, German and Danish councils of economic advisers and the British Institute for Fiscal Studies. In these cases, politicians were often wanting to signal that they were referring to more "applied" economists.

Table 2.1 Top ten economists or schools cited positively by politicians

Name of economist/school	Number of politicians	Number of references
Keynes[1]	26	59
Liberal[2]	17	29
Marx	8	19
Hayek	8	10
Free market	8	8
Adam Smith	7	12
Friedman	7	10
Council of "economic advisers"[3]	7	9
Ludwig Erhard	5	12
Danish, Scandinavian[4]	4	11

Notes:

[1]Keynes, Keynesian, Keynesianism, also post-Keynes, left Keynes.

[2]Liberal, liberalism; only when context refers to economics – i.e. not to an overall political stance.

[3]The three national councils mentioned are the Council of Economic Experts (Germany), the Council of Economic Advisers (United States) and the Economic Council (Denmark, chaired by professors known colloquially as "wise men", or even "wizards").

[4]This category literally includes "Danish" or "Scandinavian" used in front of the word "economist". Named economists are coded separately. The more common use of "Danish economists" than, for example, "French economists" or "British economists" may reflect (a) interviewees seeing Danish economists as a united "brotherhood" (see Chapter 5) or (b) the interviewee believing a non-Danish interviewer will not know the names of individual economists because they are less well known internationally than, for example, German economists such as Ludwig Erhard or French economists such as Jacques Rueff.

positive references to. Many of the economists, such as Thomas Piketty and Paul Krugman, who are listed here positively, also appear as neutral or negative mentions from the politicians we have already seen who think they have abandoned their "neutrality".

Conclusion

In interviews conducted in 2020–21, politicians' attention to economists and respect for them is patchy, low and declining. This chapter draws mostly on the three-quarters of politicians who do mention economists. Although some of them see economists as objective and adding value on the basis of their objectivity, a larger number do not. And even more common than criticism for

Table 2.2 Top twenty-first-century economists positively cited by politicians

Name	Number of politicians	Number of references
Behavioural economists[1]	4	5
Green, ecological/environmentalist[2]	4	5
German Institute for Economics	4	4
Thomas Piketty	4	9
Alternative economic policy/strategy[3]	3	5
Larry Summers	3	4
Kate Raworth	3	3
Paul Krugman	3	3
Jean Pisani-Ferry	2	3
Stephanie Stantcheva	2	3
Mariana Mazzucato	2	2
Progressive	2	2
Michael Hüther	2	2
Tony Atkinson	2	2
Robert Rubin	2	2
Republican	2	2

Notes:

[1] I include "behavioural economists" as twenty-first-century economists because most politicians mentioning them think they are very new.

[2] Where context implies recent.

[3] This is referred to by both German and British far-left politicians, so may be referring to two different strands of thought.

lack of objectivity is criticism for excessive technicality, abstraction and lack of reactivity to the fast-moving pace of real-world events.

Even those politicians who listen closely to economists see themselves, not economists, as "responsible", in the sense of shouldering responsibility. This definition of responsibility – being the decision-takers and those who will be held accountable – is more to the foreground of their thinking than the technocrats' preoccupation with responsible government as being defined by taking a long-term view and operating in the interests of all.

Their partiality – the fact that so many say only one group of economists are useful to them rather than economists as a whole – is striking. As Table 2.1, the table of quantitative references, shows, Keynes is the most positively referenced economist, followed by a very different group of politicians who cite "liberal" schools and an even more distinct group citing Marx. This divergence reflects the fact that they do not see economic experts as being as objective and united as scientific experts. It also indicates how – returning to the technocrats' plea for them to listen more to experts – they would be unlikely to be able to agree about *which* economic experts to listen to. In fact, politicians do not show themselves likely to respond positively to demands that they consult economic experts more or surrender some of their control to them. Some say they "listen" to economists and think their colleagues should listen more, but this is not one of the more dominant themes. It is significant that in confidential interviews about economic ideas and policy they do not take the opportunity to call for a bigger role for experts or want the responsibility to be taken away from them.

3

Politicians' relationships with voters

> President Clinton taught her "that campaigns are really about people's lives, and if you don't understand people's lives you can't do good policy-making".
> (Centrist Democrat)

> Ah, well. I ... think that today there is perhaps a bit of pedagogical work to be done to start with. Because ... there is a rise in populism.
> (French Socialist)

A degree of responsiveness to voters is necessary in a representative democracy (Dahl 1971). But the key reason that economic technocrats think politicians should cede control to experts is that they are *too* "responsive" to voters, who have short-term rather than long-term perspectives and do not know enough to judge what is in the interests of all. Economic technocrats see voters as forcing politicians away from delivering policy that is "responsible". What views do politicians in the five countries share about their relationships with voters and the effects these have on their ability to deliver responsible economic policy? This chapter shows how close the relationship is: politicians see voters as "the sea in which we swim". But it also shows that, as practitioners, politicians have insights into voters that go beyond the one-dimensional version of "giving in to voters' demands" that tends to underpin the technocratic arguments.

"Understandably" self-interested voters

A starting point is to ask politicians what they think about voters when it comes to the economy. Do they think voters demand self-interested policies? I asked the general question "How do you think voters see the economy?".

I expected that some at least would segment groups of voters in their answers, claiming that some groups see it differently from others. But, instead, they nearly all felt comfortable with staying with the idea of voters in the aggregate, as the question had phrased it. In addition, nearly every politician, regardless of nationality or ideology, answered that voters see the economy through the lens of their own well-being – effectively, that they *are* narrowly self-interested. There was greater unanimity on this issue than on any other question I asked. A centrist Republican says: "I mean, voters tend to look through the economy in terms of how it's impacting them directly – right? And so, how are their pay cheques – you know, are they ... rising, are they falling, is their neighbour out of a job?" A centrist Danish politician says that, "when it comes to the economy, voters will basically just want things to work". She does not think they are interested in the "economic system", but they will want it to work predictably enough that, if they "act properly, do the things [they're] supposed to do", they "can have a good life". A French centre-right politician says that "there's something which seems obvious but which I took a bit of time to discover, as an elected official. It's that the voters are fundamentally selfish." A British Conservative says they gather their information about employment patterns through local observation: "I think most people, understandably, have a view on the economy based on their own circumstance or their own experience in their everyday life, whether that is ... walking down the street and seeing curtains closed and people out of work or whether you see people in brand-new cars." But note that he says the way they base their view of the economy on their own circumstances is "understandable". A German left politician echoes this sentiment when he says that "voters see the economy primarily from their own wallet" but "I don't even mean that negatively in the sense of they're all so terribly selfish, but *of course* they ask right away: 'What impact does that have on me?'" Most politicians agree with him, and there is virtually no judgement or criticism of voters for being self-interested, although a Danish left politician does think the tendency to self-interest has become more prevalent in recent years.

Voters' preoccupation with their own circumstances precludes them paying attention to a national or supranational level. As a French centre-right politician says, voters are "without any vision of economic schools of thought, you see, of economic ideas, and without any vision of what the economic situation was like at the national level or at the international level". Many elaborate that, if voters believe their employment shows the economy is doing well, they will not pay it much attention as an issue, but, when unemployment or another indicator worsens, they will become more attentive. As a US Democrat puts it: "If they're employed and [enjoying] good jobs and doing well – yeah, the economy is doing well ... If they're unemployed and having trouble making ends meet, it's in the ground. It's in a hole. We got to get it going. Where are our political leaders when we need their help?"

Qualified judgements about voters' lack of economic understanding

A dominant strand in economics is to assert voters' economic "ignorance" (Walstad & Rebeck 2002; Caplan 2007), often on the basis of empirical fact tests. In all the interviews, not a single politician uses the word "ignorant" about voters. I argue that the second common feature of the way politicians talk about the *level* of voters' economic understanding is that it is with some respect. In a few of the interviews I asked "Is voters' lack of understanding ever an impediment?", thinking there might have been times that they were frustrated that they could not explain a complex policy they thought was necessary. The interviewees I used this wording with strongly objected to my referring to voters as an "impediment". A German CDU/CSU politician says, "It's a strong word, 'impediment', for those people who should govern us in a democratic state. So, voters are not an impediment. They are the ones we are doing this for, and so they, rightfully, are the guys who have to be represented, and they are, basically, the ones who decide about the fate of a nation."

As one British Labour politician says: "Voters are the sea in which we swim." This is echoed by a British Conservative, who states plainly, "Voters are what it's all about. They're the customers." It is as if part of the socialization of a person who becomes a politician is to start to see every person as a potential supporter who the politician must attempt to win over. Politicians who entered politics late in life from different professions affirm how much they change their outlook to orientate themselves to constantly think about seeking election and re-election. Part of this process involves them learning to see voters in the aggregate, rather than automatically segmenting off sections they will not bother to appeal to, and part of it involves talking about them with some respect. Although there are some nuanced criticisms, which I outline below, very few interviewees use the opportunity of a private interview to make sweeping condemnations of the low levels of voters' economic knowledge.

Unlike many social scientists and commentators, politicians even seem reluctant to make the milder judgement of voters as not ignorant but "lacking understanding". They often make claims that, despite voters' narrow self-interest, they understand what is happening at a common-sense level. For instance, a French Socialist politician talking about the complexity of the 2008 financial crisis comments that voters "perfectly know what's going on". It is striking how few claim that, even when voters have rejected their goals, they have done so out of a "lack of understanding". A British Remain-supporting

Conservative believes that the broadcast media often assume people do not understand and patronize them:

> We shouldn't talk about voters as if they were some lumpen mass. That's completely wrong. In any political party's set of voters, you have a wide variety of perceptions and views, and there are some people whose backgrounds are quite limited but who are very shrewd about the big picture. And they may talk about it in quite basic ways, but they grasp the essence of it quite clearly.

Here, in his reference to people whose backgrounds are "limited" but who are "shrewd", he is presenting voters as being preoccupied with their own circumstances but nevertheless capable of making common-sense judgements about the bigger picture when necessary. One Liberal Democrat Remain supporter does suggest voters did not share his beliefs about what was economically beneficial, or became "wrongly" convinced by some of the Leave campaign message that the economic harm would not be significant. But most Remain-supporting interviewees believe Leave voters voted the way they did because they wanted to take back control, not because they did not understand economic issues. One Conservative former minister says the explanation for the Leave victory "was not that [Leave voters] lacked some economic understanding". Instead, he came to the conclusion, "having studied it quite carefully", that "they didn't care about potential economic harm". He cites one voter in an industry that many argued would suffer from leaving the European Union saying that, "even if you absolutely can prove to me that I'm going to lose not only my job but the jobs of others, I'm still in favour of this because it's the right thing to do". The politician comments about this voter, "It was not lack of information, nor even lack of trust in information received. It was a view apparently honourable. Indeed, in this case, a self-sacrificing view." His Conservative Remain colleague says that the economic costs and benefits of membership of the European Union was a "complex" issue, which boils down to your "instinctive" approach to it. Although his use of the term "complex" indicates that he thinks there might have been some lack of understanding, he is not critical of an "instinctive" approach. British Conservatives are some of the least likely to mention voters as "lacking understanding".

However, a substantial number of politicians go on to express beliefs that show they do think voters have limited economic understanding, even if they tend to express them in careful and qualified ways. A French centre-right politician comes close to a claim of lack of understanding when she says "I learned from experience that voters are very little informed". A German former AfD politician who has high respect for (ordoliberal) economics acknowledges that, "in general, I have to say that it is of course extremely difficult to understand economics. It is simply difficult to see this entanglement, this complexity." He finds it easier to explain his pro-market message to "people who had worked in the fresh air or who were now directly involved in the market". These people with direct experience of markets "understood immediately, even if the issues were very complicated", compared with people who "tend to have lived in their rooms or not known real life", such as teachers.

Some French and American politicians are more likely to be concerned about some voters having such "simplistic" understanding that they become susceptible to "populism". All the interviewees who mention populism as a term are critical of it (although note that far-right populist parties are under-represented). Only one, a French Socialist, uses "populist" for the left wing, in this case the party La France insoumise. The rest focus exclusively on far-right populist politicians, saying they either downplay or over-simplify economic issues, as in the comment that "these are parties where economic discourse is going to show through very, very little". A second French politician, also on the left, believes many voters have become more "sceptical", and this is accentuated by economic fear during the pandemic: "People's thinking is organized around fear of these [economic] subjects, around anxiety about these topics. Thus that limits understanding hugely." This politician argues that all voters care about is whether policies will "work"; they have become very practical and pragmatic. This makes it even harder for politicians, whether on the left or the right, to try to explain the complexities and unpredictability of economic policy. There is a "failure of reflection, and of constructive debate around economic policy". France has (only just) avoided keeping support for populists low enough to keep them out of government, and I show in Chapter 6 that French politicians are more pessimistic about voters' willingness to engage with economic debate than those in other countries. There are echoes of this in the United States, as I show in Chapter 7, where many Republicans privately criticize Donald Trump, on the grounds that, as president, he tried to appeal to voters desperate for simple solutions and took economic policy in a simplistic and populist direction.

The first part of responsiveness: listening to voters

Responsiveness is usually defined as the process of politicians following or anticipating public opinion (Erikson, MacKuen & Stimson 2002). A necessary first stage is that they have to listen to voters. But even the act of politicians listening may involve more than is often recognized. Politicians have to learn to be empathetic listeners, which involves learning how to see the economy the way their constituents do. A British Conservative says he has always enjoyed listening to voters, "because it's listening to what their stated concerns are, but also what their unstated concerns are, and then trying to answer that in a way that answers both their stated and unstated concerns". A British Labour politician, a former minister, says: "I think this is where you come to the heart of things in the discussion we're having; people elect their politicians or MPs to represent them, and if you're going to represent people you've got to see the world as most people see it, not through the eyes of distinguished economists."

Nearly all politicians raise a further benefit to listening closely to their constituents: that they learn from them about economic conditions on the ground. We have seen in Chapter 2 that politicians argue that economists are sometimes too far removed from real-world conditions. The economist adviser in Chapter 2 who was close to British ministers during the 2008 financial crisis and had a high opinion of the skills politicians brought to bear on the crisis describes their distinctive contribution to an emergency council consisting of both economists and politicians. He says the politicians think "not only what's going to work [economically], but how's this playing in my constituency, how's it playing in the North?" The politicians were getting constant and immediate feedback from their constituents and comparing notes with other politicians in the tea room. The politicians were also preoccupied with communication strategies, and the informed and effective communication in itself had positive economic effects, by calming people.

Whereas in reality some politicians may also spend a lot of time listening to lobbyists, a centrist Democrat in the United States explains that the economic intelligence he gets from Main Street is different from what he gets from Wall Street lobbyists: "And you have to really walk down Main Street to gauge and ask people how they feel the economy. The one Main Street of any city US of A, I think, will give you a very good gauge." A British Conservative remembers Britain's exit from the exchange rate mechanism in 1992, which he strongly supported. He was strengthened in his resolve when listening to a constituent:

> I remember on one of those nights a constituent crossing the road to talk to me, showing me the keys to his business. He said, "Do you see these? I'm about to put them into the bank. I'm about to tell the bank I can't run my business if you keep these interest rates as high as they are. I need you to know that." And I said, "You have made it very visible and firm to me and I will double my efforts."

He says that this constituent was reinforcing a position he had already taken, but he adds that, if constituents keep giving you local information about damage to their businesses caused by a policy you support, then you should consider "changing your mind".

The second part of responsiveness: "persuading"

We should not see responsiveness as stopping at the end of the first stage of politicians' listening. Scholars writing about the need for technocracy tend to define politician "responsiveness" simply as responding to "the demands" of voters. For instance, Daniele Caramani (2020) defines responsiveness in this way in the introduction to an edited volume while, in the conclusion, Eri Bertsou (2020) writes about responsiveness as "to the demands of the people" (247) or "to the demands of any given majority" (249). This is a one-dimensional picture. Other scholars, such as Jane Mansbridge (2003) and Lisa Disch (2011), remind us that the picture is more rounded, involving two-way communication. Part of responsiveness also involves politicians attempting to shape voters' demands, and voters' perceptions of whether they have responded to them. As Peter Esaiasson and Christopher Wlezien (2017: 702) recognize, politicians also attempt to "explain" their actions to voters.

All the politicians interviewed thought communicating with voters was important. A British economist adviser says that "you want the politicians to in some ways have an instinct about how to present and sell" economic messages and policies. An American Democrat says that the job of the politician is "not to be the academic economist, and it's not to be the CEO, but it is to take those elements and to learn, listen really well, gain trust, and to *communicate*". Many politicians talk about how they translate economists' ideas into viable policies, but they also talk about translating the policies into "stories" for voters. Politicians have had to learn how to communicate in their months on campaign trails. A Trump-supporting Republican says he represents a poor district with a high proportion living in trailers, but he has been talking to them so long he thinks he has learned to communicate, and they understand him.

Mansbridge's (2003) work on responsiveness as a two-way process comes closer to giving the degree of emphasis politicians give to the communicating part of responsiveness. A further benefit is that she identifies standards of communication, arguing that we both can and should judge the *quality* of how politicians attempt to persuade voters. At the lowest level of communicative quality, Mansbridge argues that some politicians attempt to deceive or manipulate voters. No interviewees openly admit to intending to deceive voters. Some former United Kingdom Independence Party (UKIP) politicians describe a process that could be interpreted as manipulating voters. One former UKIP politician admits that, in the Brexit campaign, "economics was sort of subservient to the overall politics and strategic aim of UKIP, but nonetheless was an important way of driving all those [Eurosceptic Labour voters] to us". Coming up to the 2015 general election, UKIP was divided over its economic goals but knew that it needed to present a united front to voters, and so decided to choose the economic policies that would be most popular with their target voters: Eurosceptics who usually voted Labour. In previous elections the UKIP leadership, consisting largely of "Thatcherites",[1] had not produced economic policies favourable to the National Health Service (NHS), such as pledging spending increases. But in 2015 this UKIP politician persuaded the leadership to insert a pledge to spend what he describes as the "big notional savings from the EU annual subscription" on the NHS. He says that he told them: "Now, if you're aiming at a blue-collar electorate of mainly older voters who've paid their national insurance stamps for 30 years, they're going to want the offer of the NHS to be there for them. So, again, I think I managed to sell that certainly [*sic*] pragmatically [to the UKIP leadership]." Note that he sold it "pragmatically". Their communication to these sceptical voters to spend on the NHS can be described as manipulative, given that it is unlikely that the leadership would have introduced the policy.

I do not think we should rush to judgement here, or assume that, just because some former UKIP politicians were the only ones who admitted to manipulating, that other politicians who did not admit it in interviews did not come close. For instance, politicians who believe the state's finances are equivalent to those of a household, hence justifying a debt-averse stance, are not deceiving voters. However, some interviewees, including Conservatives, suggest that leading politicians from their party pushed the household analogy message during the post-2008 austerity period to voters even though they did not believe it. In addition, the "low" standard of communication should not just consist of manipulative messages. If we return to how the former UKIP politician describes economic issues as secondary, we could argue that attempts to downplay economic issues by overemphasizing cultural, political or social issues amounts to a form of manipulation. The US politicians in particular argue that the recent preoccupation of some politicians with culture has crowded out how much attention voters have left for dryer, harder-to-understand economic issues.

For Mansbridge (2003), the higher-quality politician communication standard involves "clarifying" and "explaining", obviously without any intention to deceive. This can be summarized as "educating". "Educating" may involve challenging how voters think. Whether politician interviewees currently attempt to educate seems to depend in part on their personal predisposition. Some politicians see it as part of their mission. In some cases, these politicians were

---

1. By "Thatcherite", this politician means followers of Margaret Thatcher, the UK's Conservative prime minister from 1979 to 1990, who promoted policies of low taxation and low government spending.

teachers or even economics lecturers before they became politicians, and the desire to educate has continued. But, in cases in which they did not have this professional background, the predisposition to educate seems to be a random characteristic. However, the degree of *pressure* to educate is a significant factor. When there is more pressure, politicians, whatever their predisposition, make greater effort. Pressure depends on whether politicians' economic beliefs are swimming with or against the dominant voter beliefs in the country. I give examples of when politicians feel pressure to educate because they are swimming against the tide first. Then I follow with examples of the opposite case; when politicians feel less pressure to educate, they may even prefer to do as little economic "educating" as possible, because voters' perceptions are already in line with their own.

Politicians feel pressure to educate about their economic policies when they run counter to dominant voter beliefs that are usually long held. The household debt analogy, a widely held belief across voters in the five countries, is a case in point. In this, the nation's finances are seen as analogous to those of a household. Thus, just as any household getting into debt will eventually face punishment in the shape of bankruptcy, house dispossession, and so on, a government that gets into debt must face similarly damaging consequences. But some economists, such as Keynes, argued that a government's greater ability to issue bonds and borrow, and to borrow in anticipation that investment may yield higher tax revenues from growth in future, means it is *not* analogous to a household. Many politicians who do not believe in the household debt analogy, and want to increase spending and borrowing for investment, find strong resistance to their views from voters who have a long-standing commitment to the household debt analogy because it builds on their own experience. A British centrist who thinks a special case for borrowing to invest needs to be made complains how hard it was to explain this to voters: "I think there is a lot of scepticism around the word 'borrowing'. It sounds very profligate, left. I think a lot of people worry about it." As I show in Chapter 5 on Denmark and Germany, most German right-wing politicians are strongly debt-averse. German politicians on the left and within the Green party say they have found it hard to challenge the household debt analogy when they have wanted to increase investment, such as on infrastructure. A German Green politician is "depressed" by how easy it is for "these right-wing people [to] get through with their [debt-averse] message". In Germany the household debt analogy is often referred to as embodying the values of the "Schwabian hausfrau", which the Green politician describes as "a story so old still we are not able to destroy it on the communication level". A German far-left politician says it is easier to politicize and argue for wealth taxation and the right to full employment than it is to counter the aversion to debt, which he describes as a more "complicated" endeavour. These politicians have no choice but to constantly attempt to edu-cate voters about how the state is different and why borrowing to invest might even reduce debt in the long term. In this case, none of them have ground breaking suggestions for how to do that effectively, other than by repetition.

Second, an eclectic group of "economic liberal" politicians complain that they feel pressure to "clarify" and "educate". These are "economic liberals" in France, Denmark and Germany, who are in despair as to what they call the "default tendency" of voters to be "anti-market". I give further details about how tough it is to be an economic liberal in those countries in Chapter 5 and 6. But, to take one example here, a German politician who sees himself on the economically liberal wing of the CDU/CSU says about "the German popula-tion right now" – as many other German right-wingers did – that "there's a great distrust in liberal and pro-market ideas at all". Advocating for lower tax and welfare spending is "very hard": "So, I think we need to explain to the voter what we're doing, why we're doing it. But it's easier for those people who are offering simple solutions, such as 'We're raising taxes'. … It's an easy way to sell yourself, as a politician; it's much easier than to talk about the more obscure, harder truth David Ricardo and Adam Smith have to offer."

Third, free traders, particularly in the United States, feel pressure to "clarify" and "educate". A centrist Republican who opposed some of President Trump's economic policies, such as on trade, says the protectionist message is "always easier to communicate", to the extent that he calls it a "populist standpoint". A centrist Democrat, who was also a free trader, describes asking eco-nomic advisers for data she could use. She says the free trade debates were a "nightmare", provoking a "visceral reaction" in her district. These debates were the "hardest", and, "frankly, the academics can provide you with some ammunition for that, but, ultimately, you have to translate that, and turn that into a story". A second free trade Republican says he would raise protectionism at "town hall meetings", which many of the American interviewees describe holding on a regular basis. He found that, once the Trump tariffs on steel and aluminium had passed, it actually became easier to get across the message about their harmful effects. Effectively, they helped him educate the voters, becoming "a good communication point". Nevertheless, free trade still takes a long time and effort to explain.

For the opposite politicians, those swimming *with* the tide, reputations for sound economic competence reduce pressure to educate. British Conservatives constitute one group who give the impression that they do not have to work hard on messaging, because the public are pro-free-market and the media are on their side. A former Conservative minister is insightful as to why voters are receptive to their messages. He says, "First of all, I think voters do care about the economy. It's not by any means the only thing that they care about. But

I think they are inclined to vote for governments that have economic credibility in the eyes of the voter; whether they're right or wrong is another matter."

Here he implies it is the Conservatives who have the "credibility". In fact, he says it's rare that "the British public have voted in an economically reckless way", which implies that in the recent past only New Labour[2] has temporarily had some credibility. Because voters know what their own self-interests and circumstances are, they will draw on that to make the necessary judgement about which party is credible. He concludes that, because of this ability to go from their own circumstances to work out what policies might work at the national level, "I think they've probably got a reasonably good sense, by and large, as to whether a politician sounds credible on the economy".

A second Conservative former minister expands on what voters understand about the economy. He is careful not to sound disrespectful to voters but says their level of understanding is not "sophisticated". They sometimes find it difficult to understand statistics: "You actually realize that you've got to be quite careful how you put things across to people, because, if you are explaining something in a way that they don't really comprehend, then you're wasting your time, and indeed you will create a sense of frustration in them." Therefore, Conservatives do not have to put much effort into "clarifying". Note that attempting to educate may even make voters feel "frustrated". Instead, they need to deliver enough of a sense that voters' own economic circumstances are improving or will improve under "credible" government, and the voter will tend to interpret that as meaning they should vote Conservative. As a third Conservative comments, it is only when the Conservatives make (rare) economic mistakes, such as over the European Union's Exchange Rate Mechanism policy in the early 1990s, that voters stop thinking they are credible.

It is not only the right that feels lack of voter pressure to educate. In Denmark the centrist and left-of-centre parties have it easy. A centrist politician who tried to introduce welfare reforms to cut taxes illustrates this. Voters were so resistant to the reforms, despite Denmark having the highest tax burden in the world, that eventually his party gave up. He says, "Some Danes said, 'But why, why, do you want to continue to do reforms?' Voters turned against reform, saying: 'Now you reform, reform, reform, we have reform fatigue; we don't want more reforms now; just leave us alone.' And at that point we couldn't explain why to do it." Those further to the left in Denmark are not surprised. A far-left politician says that for the last 20 or so years right-wing parties have not been able to win elections on the basis of their

---

2. "New Labour" is the term often used for the only period of Labour government (1997 to 2010) in the last 40 years.

economic policies: "I would say that, at least in Danish politics, the narrative of welfare system and the narrative of strong trade unions and the value of having organized labour, so to speak, I think is really broad." Interestingly, he sounds like a British Conservative when he prefaces these remarks with the comment "Very few voters study economics, of course", which implies that he thinks one key factor is that the pro-welfare and pro-tax narrative is already so dominant that it does not take much effort on the part of left parties to bolster it up and gain support for their economic policies. A Danish Social Democrat politician characterizes voters as "lacking a technical grasp". Like British Conservatives, he sounds relatively complacent about this, because they do not need a technical grasp to understand pro-welfare arguments that are long-standing, seen as common sense, in his country.

Conclusion

Are economic technocrats right that politicians' responsiveness to voters undermines responsible government, because voters are short-termist and do not back policies in the interests of all? This chapter started by showing that, at first glance, politicians apparently agree with technocrats, because they judge voters to be "narrowly self-interested". But, although technocrats argue that a crucial explanation as to why voters are short-termist and self-interested is that they do not understand enough of the complexities, one of the reasons they tend to push for technocracy in "technical" and complex policy areas, politicians do not make that part of the argument. Politicians seem to "respect" voters, including most of them not being prepared to make sweeping judgements about their "lack of understanding". Politicians characterize voter self-interest as "understandable" rather than directly criticizing it as a limitation.

But is politicians' respect for voters a form of socialization that is in reality superficial, even false, a way of behaving that makes it more likely politicians will not slip up and show lack of respect to the voters they need to win over? Or is it more genuine? On the side of there being an element of falseness, many politicians may not make the sweeping judgement of a "lack of understanding", but they go on, in the detail of their answers, to talk about how hard it is to explain some complex issues, and, in some cases, how voters would benefit from more civics or economic education. On the side of politicians' respect for voters being more genuine, they see voters as a source of information about what is happening economically on the ground, and indicate that they gain a lot from listening to them. These interviews are confidential, and some of the interviewees are deeply concerned about the populist threat. Yet they sound genuinely annoyed when they think I am being condescending towards voters. Perhaps the clue to this somewhat uneasy position is a certain shyness on the part of the politicians. We have seen in Chapter 2 that politicians care deeply about their often moral economic goals. Yet they believe voters are completely economically self-interested. When they talk to voters, is there a kind of deception as they try to meet voters by toning down the morality of what they believe? This tension is greater when it comes to economic issues, because voters are more likely to be on the same moral wavelength as politicians when it comes to social and foreign policy issues.

Politicians do not often explicitly raise their responsiveness to voters as leading them to dilute policies so that they are no longer "responsible". They may try to present themselves in the best light, so it would be surprising if they raised it proactively as a judgement on themselves. Nevertheless, there are a few examples. A British Green politician, for example, is consistently respectful towards voters throughout her interview. Her party has been thinking about radical modern monetary policy proposals. She herself is not convinced, but part of her hesitation concerns persuading voters. She says that, when you adopt an economic policy, you have to start from "where the public are": "Therefore, you know, if you come in and you basically say to them 'Look, I know that you are really worried about not having enough money to live on, but we are going to change the entire banking system and the whole way in which we do money creation', they just look at you as if to say 'What's that got to do with my life?'" As a result, her conclusion is that her party should not adopt the policy until they have developed a way of talking about it that is more "concrete". However, the crucial point here is that she will consider finding a way of talking to voters about this policy.

This chapter has introduced the notion that politicians should "educate" voters about economic issues, a subject I return to after exploring the ideological and national variations in politicians' relationships with economists and voters.

PART II

Ideological and national variations

Part I shows some overall patterns in how politicians think about economists and voters across the five countries. In Part II I explore some of the ideological and national differences. I have had to take an asymmetric approach. If I had focused on a chapter for each country, it would have exaggerated the extent of national differences. I found that the centre and far-left interviewees across all five countries shared enough to warrant separating them out in a chapter on "the left".

I selected the five countries on the basis that they reflected varieties of capitalism and varieties of style of democracy. Attitudes to economists seemed to vary according to the degree to which a country had a consensual political system, usually most obviously characterized by features such as frequent coalition government. It is beyond the descriptive nature of this book to ascertain whether the style of democracy is what *causes* the attitudes to economists. Other factors, such as economic conditions or intellectual cultures, may be equally important. I just note that there was a correlation. Therefore, I have grouped Denmark and Germany together, and, similarly, the two pluralist cases of the United Kingdom and the United States. However, the French interviewees were distinct in their attitudes to economists in a number of key respects, so they deserve a chapter on their own.

The final chapter in this section focuses on one aspect of politicians' thinking: the economics of the environment. This chapter attempts to justify the stance taken throughout the book, that at least for the moment it is impossible to understand politicians' attitudes to the economics of the environment without first understanding their attitudes to economic ideas more generally – the main subject of the book. In the same way, we cannot understand their attitude to economists who write on the environment without knowing that broader context first.

4

The resurgent left's view of economists

Socialists take a good deal of inspiration from Keynesians.

(French Socialist politician)

I have always seen the economy as a contested, also politically contested, field, in which the different social interests of different population groups meet. And I have held on to this kind of thinking to this day, and actually find it confirmed in many ways.

(German Die Linke politician)

I have combined the left from all five countries because of how much they share. Their right-wing counterparts tend to follow more nationally rooted paths, which I cover in the next chapters. This chapter illustrates three themes. The first theme is the divergence in economic ideas, driven by the left. Much of the existing research into politicians' economic goals and policy-making was conducted at the height of the neoliberal era, when many argue that centre-left goals were becoming more similar to those on the right, converging on a pro-market stance (Berman 2006; Mudge 2011, 2018). But many of these interviewees argue that, since the 2008 financial crisis, they have moved to the left (see also Manwaring & Holloway 2022). There is an increasing confidence that leftist economic ideas are gaining a wider audience, although, perhaps not unsurprisingly, left-wing politicians in Europe show greater confidence than progressive Democrats in the United States.

The second theme is how politicians on the left respect economists, but only if they belong to a particular strand of thinking. There are crucial differences between the attitudes of centre-[1] and far-left[2] interviewees towards economists. The centre left often follows "Keynesian" approaches, while the far left follows a mix of economists but only if they are in the heterodox category, outside the mainstream. The far-left politicians are, arguably, paying closer attention to economists than their centre-left counterparts. The differences in *which* economists are respected reinforces the point that politicians would find it difficult to follow a technocratic path involving ceding control to economic experts in general.

Finally, many commentators have seen the left as generally more opposed to ceding control over economic policy to experts than the right. I find that the left still seems to believe that, in the current time, economic policy should continue to be contested in the political domain.

I cover the left in the United States, the UK and Germany in depth, with some reference to the French and Danish, but there are also some nationally specific points to make about the French and Danish left in Chapters 5 and 6. I cover the left's economic thinking about the environment in Chapter 8.

The moral nature of left-wing politicians' economic goals

Traditionally, the left has been characterized as having more moral or normative economic goals than the right. Most left-wing politicians talk about how a desire for social justice brought them into politics. A couple mention religion, such as the German Green whose interest in the Catholic poor movement turned into a long-standing commitment to the "justice question in economics". But most recount early family experiences or observations rather than religion. A Danish Social Democrat has had the desire for a "just and relatively

---

1. I categorize politicians I interviewed from these parties as "centre left" in economic terms: non-Corbynite British Labour, German SPD, German Greens (whatever their radicalism on environmental issues, German Greens themselves describe their party's economic ideas as closer to the SPD's than the far left's), French Socialist, Danish Social Democrats (although the Danish Social Democrats do also figure prominently in the "national" chapter covering Denmark: 5) and American Democrats. I categorize them as centre left rather than far left partly on the basis of their own use of the categories during the interviews.

2. I categorize politicians I interviewed from these parties as "far left" in economic terms: Die Linke, Corbynite Labour, British Greens, Danish Red–Green Alliance (De Rød–Grønne), Danish Alternative (Alternativet) and French Communist Party (Parti communiste français: PCF). I categorize them as far left partly on the basis of their own use of the categories during the interviews.

equal society" since his teens, which he says has never changed. The chapter on Denmark includes many more examples of politicians whose main motive in economic policy is maintaining a high level of welfare because of the belief that this is the morally right thing to do and likely to lead to the benefit of a socially harmonious society. Left politicians often talk about having economic values that stem from their broader beliefs in human rights. For instance, a French Socialist uses the term "solidarity", which he believes encompasses respect for human rights:

> So, for me, these are the fundamental values: respect for the individual, for man, his liberty, dignity, the fight against inequality and from now on the fight for the planet, a state which is a bit less bad for future generations. So, there you go; those are the very deep values which converge around the question of solidarity. You don't just think of yourself, but of those who are coming behind.

A German Social Democrat echoes a common tendency to use the term "goals" often in the interviews. She says that you have to look at your own principles, ask yourself "Where do you want to go?", and that it was always clear to her that "my goal is a socially just society".

These values of social justice underpin left politicians' economic beliefs. They tend to think that the values of justice conditioned their approach to economic policy, rather than the other way round. An American Democrat says that her economic values, her goal of distributive justice, drives her approach to economic ideas about which policies might work: "My ideas are in absolute alignment with my values ... my values were ... in my core, and I always look for policy solutions that are in line with my values." A French Socialist became very interested in economic policy, but she describes her economic values as coming first: "I was interested in the economy because I thought that was the way to have a fair society. That was my entry point." This means that they tend to see "the economy" as less of an autonomous sphere than economists do, and more as a tool for shaping society. A Danish far-left politician says his goals are social. He wants "the economy to become a tool to create a society where all people can live and have a good life and where we take care of the planet at the same time. So, economics is a tool and not in itself a goal at all."

European confidence and American timidity

Politicians on the left express confidence in their economic ideas, giving the impression that they think they are in tune with the spirit of the times.

A British far-left adviser says that "the bias of British politics towards the left on economics is strikingly more now than it was five years ago". To contextualize this confidence, how do they see what many argue was a convergence of ideas in the neoliberal era, when the centre left in particular shifted in a market-conforming direction? The German SPD and centrist British Labour politicians tend not to dwell on it. One SPD politician raises it and calls it "neoliberal" by name, saying "Ah, yes, we had a very long phase of neoliberalism in Germany too", which was responsible for undercutting wages. She says that most of the SPD now no longer wants it.

The far-left politicians raise the neoliberal turn more often and are critical. A German far-left politician who is prominent in developing an alternative economic policy says it is no coincidence the group was first formed in 1975, as the centre left switched into what he describes as the "Helmut Schmidt era" of a different kind of economics. In the UK, far-left politicians on the Corbynite wing of the Labour Party and the Greens take it for granted that the more neoliberal path their New Labour colleagues took was a mistake.

The centre left expresses confidence in the dominance of its economic ideas at the current time. Many imply that this confidence has been building since the 2008 financial crisis proved the case for more regulation that they had been making. In addition, their confidence is on the whole boosted by the pandemic. Although some have fears about a potentially negative relationship between the pandemic and environmentalist economic policies, and many raise the greater suffering of those on low incomes in terms of poorer health outcomes and their key worker status, most think the pandemic will make voters more accepting of the case for state intervention. At the time of the interviews, from February 2020 to December 2021, economic conditions were shifting rapidly, so most were careful not to predict too confidently. But here is a typical example from the far left about how some economic attitudes might have shifted long term. A British Green says that what is interesting about the pandemic is that, "when the crisis hits, everybody knows that only the government can sort this out". What she describes as the "Reaganite lie" – that governments cannot sort out crises – has been "blown apart". She despairs that war has often been the catalyst for "transformative" economic change, but she sees this crisis as similar to a war. A centre-left British adviser says that both the current Conservative government and voters now understand that it may make good economic sense to borrow in order to invest, an argument that centre-left governments had trouble making around the time of the 2008 financial crisis. Far-left Danish interviewees express some frustration that so many Danish politicians and voters have tended to be debt-averse. They believe the pandemic may have shifted thinking in this respect. One says the Social Democrat government is currently increasing the deficit: "I think that will also change something in the debate for a long time to come. If it's just big enough, wild enough, and serious enough, then we can actually exceed what the right-wing side think is nature's law regarding economic policy." Another far-left Danish politician expresses a common sentiment that the Biden stimulus package is a return to "Keynesian" ideas about the role of the state. He believes this is proof that neoliberal ideas are now in a "defensive" position, with "social democratic ideas playing offence".

However, in contrast to their European counterparts, I find that US Democrats are less optimistic and confident that their economic ideas are going to become dominant. There has been much commentary on "Bidenomics" (Brownstein 2021), claims that economists such as Jared Bernstein, centred in the Economic Policy Institute, have persuaded the president to go in a more radical, egalitarian, pro-union and race-focused direction in economic policy compared with previous, more cautious Democrat administrations. However, these interviews give a less striking impression of a leftward economic shift. First, it is very noticeable how far centrist Democrats still are from European social democrats when it comes to the level of distributive justice that should underpin economic policy. For instance, one centrist Democrat says she supports only limited state intervention, if outcome measures show it to be effective. "New" progressive Democrats are more critical of how the current economic system works than the centrists. They distinguish themselves from centrist Democrats and "old-style" progressives by arguing for a larger scale of educational and social reforms and promoting higher wages and job security, to tackle the "gig economy". So, whereas some centrist Democrat interviewees consider it wrong that post-pandemic job vacancies are not being filled because furlough payments have introduced a culture of dependence, new progressives are more likely to say that the hospitality and other low-paid sectors had been long overdue for an overhaul. One young progressive adviser says that people in his "millennial or Z generation" think that "we need to make big investments". In addition, he wants to raise the real minimum wage. The United States is "behind" other industrialized countries on "basic" welfare entitlements such as parental leave and healthcare. He says his more centrist colleagues want to go more slowly, "little step by step", and he characterizes the main difference between them and him as "incremental versus immediate". The centrist "incrementalists" want to avoid pushing up debt. On debt, he is "not saying it's not important, but the way we talk about it is just a political hot potato, because both sides have agreed to increase the debt ceiling before; we're in that boat again". If there does have to be a drive to reduce debt, he would prefer it to be through raising taxes than cutting spending.

However, although the Democratic adviser's ideas may be described as radical and in line with what he defines as the "most progressive" section of the party, he is timid. His analysis is that Democrat economic ideas in the early days of the Biden presidency were "pushing to the left". This push started before the pandemic but has been encouraged by it. However, he is reluctant to describe his beliefs as "social democrat" or "socialist". When he says he was deeply influenced during his early socialization by the 2008 financial crisis and the injustice of bank bailouts, he rushes to add that "I'm not saying no one should ever be a billionaire, but you should pay your fair taxes" and that "obviously, I wouldn't call myself a socialist". The only Democrats who he thinks would define themselves as "European-style" "social democrats" or "socialists" are Bernie Sanders and Alexandria Ocasia-Cortez. His reluctance to ascribe those labels to himself is, in part, fear of how the Republicans use any brand with the word "social" in it to immediately paint the person as Communist, usually to great political effect. But he also believes progressives have to argue within the groove of what he calls "mythology, or the American story of independence of picking yourself up by your bootstraps and making your own way", which is still "very ingrained in our culture". He thinks that "the traditions, the concepts of what we believe in, our feelings of capitalism and the free market and individualism" will continue to prevail, and it will take "generations" to shift them.

Attitudes to economists: centre-left "Keynesianism"

In Chapter 2 we have seen that left politicians are more prone than the right to see economists as less objective than hard scientists. The centre left tends to say that, rather than supporting the discipline of economics, it supports one strand of economic thinking, in the shape of Keynesianism. Many centre-left politicians in the four European countries use the word "Keynesian" when asked to define their economic ideas, and, as we have seen in Chapter 2, this is why on a quantitative count he was the most frequently positively cited economist by far. It is important to note that only left-wing interviewees say they support "Keynes". The few on the right who say they support him do so only in the extreme and specific circumstances of, for example, investing out of a crisis such as the pandemic.

This centre-left attachment to "Keynesianism" has two main features. First, the centre-left politicians imply that their attachment may have waxed and waned, but it has always been a backdrop. Whatever their stance on the neoliberal era, the centre-left interviewees imply that they never stopped having "Keynesian" ideas as the foundation of their economic thinking. And at the current time, following the discrediting of pro-market ideas since the 2008 crisis and with most governments – whatever their ideological stance – drawing on "Keynesian" ideas in the pandemic, they seem increasingly confident in their "Keynesianism". In this respect they support scholars such as historian Jim Tomlinson (2007, 2017). A British politician describes "Keynesianism" as "coming back into fashion" from the 2008 crisis following a brief period when it may have been eclipsed, but that it was always a backdrop for him. Danish centre-left politicians imply that Keynesian ideas never went out of fashion, although more "supply-side" approaches were "integrated" with them.

German SPD politicians imply that they have undergone more of a paradigmatic shift to Keynesianism in recent years than the Danes, British or French, because they have shaken off the fiscal rules of ordoliberalism. Many scholars argue that German centre-left politicians had periods of reliance on Keynesian ideas, such as in the late 1960s and 1970s, but that these combined with a dominant ordoliberal orthodoxy at that time and then declined following the neoliberal turn in the 1980s, and the embrace of a "third way" Giddenite path (for a review, see Feld, Köhler & Nientiedt 2021). However, according to the German SPD interviewees, the party has undergone a "paradigmatic" shift to Keynesian economic ideas within the last ten years. A leading SPD politician explains that, "after the financial and global economic crisis, something changed here too, and I would like to see an even faster paradigm shift on this issue. So something has changed in my party." This is reflected in the fact that every one of the German SPD interviewees defines him- or herself as "Keynesian".

In the last couple of years, when Olaf Scholz was finance minister, many argue that the shift away from ordoliberal fiscal orthodoxy and towards Keynesianism has become more pronounced within the German economics discipline and among left politicians. Caroline de Gruyter (2021) argues that a "new generation" of economists has come to prominence, including Philippa Sigl-Glöckner, at the Dezernat Zukunft think tank, and Isabel Schnabel, on the European Central Bank board. This is reflected in the SPD interviewee's account; she goes on to say that there is beginning to be a change to a "high level of scientific discourse" (meaning among economists), with challenges to the ordoliberal debt aversity. Other German centre-left interviewees with high levels of economic training echo her in their admiration for what Keynes brings to economic theory and policy-making. Therefore, now more than ever, there seems some truth in Tomlinson's argument in relation to these five countries that Keynesianism has been there as a constant backdrop, including at the height of the neoliberal era, and even more so now given the more thoroughgoing conversion of the German SPD to a Keynesian way of thinking.

The second feature of social democrats' use of the term "Keynesianism" is how they imply that it is suited to achieving social democratic goals. When I directly ask "How do you define your economic ideas?", interestingly, those in Denmark and Germany who label themselves "Social Democrat" in terms of their overall ideological stance and party name often do not describe their economic ideas as "social democrat" but, instead, as "Keynesian". Others, such as British Labour politicians and French Socialists, also often use the word "Keynesian" to describe their economic ideas. A French Socialist says that, when it comes to "redistribution", "socialists take a good deal of inspiration from Keynesians". Usually, they use it to denote an overall stance. A second French left politician says her support for Keynes "is not only caricaturing Keynes and talking about spending money in order to support the economy. It is also Keynes' whole thought process of saying 'What is my political objective, and, based on that political objective, what type of economy do I want and how should I organize that?'" Her implication here is that other neoclassical economists do not give social democrats the scope to say that they want to pursue a goal such as full employment or redistribution, because they believe politicians should follow market forces. A French centre-left politician who is a former minister says the left that he represents, which he describes as "realist" (some others use the term "practical" or "pragmatic"), to distinguish himself from further-left idealism, "has always been Keynesian". The way he elaborates on what this means is shared by many other centre-left politicians. He says Keynes thinks that "the state can be extremely useful": "It's a vision of the working of the economy where the state has its place, and where public spending can be a good thing; it isn't in principle something problematic." This adds to what he describes as the "more progressive part" of Keynesianism, which takes on board full employment and redistribution. So, even though a few focus on one aspect, such as the good sense of stimulating demand when threatened with rising unemployment, the tendency to see Keynesianism as a holistic approach to policy is the dominant one.

This French Socialist interviewee last cited acknowledges Keynesianism encompasses many sub-schools, but he says he belongs to "Keynesianism" in the broadest sense rather than narrowing his support to one of them. In general, most centre-left politicians do not bother to mention that there are strands of Keynesian thinking, such as "neo-", or "post-" or "left-", to the same degree that far-left politicians do when they talk about "Keynesianism". Centre-left Keynesianism varies in depth, with some paying Keynes and various strands of Keynesian thought a lot of attention, and others treating "Keynes" as a shorthand term for a predisposition to state intervention to accomplish their goals, which they pursue pragmatic means to achieve.

There are differences in how the Anglosphere centre left sees Keynes compared with the French, German and Danish. First, we have already noted that US Democrats mention him less often, although none of them are critical of Keynes. One progressive Democrat uses "Keynes" as a shorthand for "more state intervention" and characterizes support for it as defining progressives' desire for "a Keynesian kind of society again [going back to pre-Reaganite times]" when "governments are the real support" in welfare terms and "put more reins on the market". Second, British centre-left politicians are slightly more offhand or non-committal as to what support for Keynes actually means. A Labour politician says, "I guess I probably would see myself in economic terms as Keynesian." But he laughs and adds: "That doesn't really help [you] very much!" They treat Keynesianism as an "approach" rather than a coherent theoretical framework. A former Labour minister says, "Keynes is a classic example if you're looking for an overall *approach*." However, this less detailed support for Keynes may reflect how, because he is a British economist, his ideas are even more of a backdrop in British politics than elsewhere.

The far left's attention, to heterodox economists only

Like the "confident Keynesians" on the centre left, there is a parallel rise in the confidence with which far-left politicians talk about their economic ideas. Their numbers are small and they are not in government, but they believe they are attracting support and exerting pressure on the centre left. The far-left politicians are contributing to the unprecedented degree of diversity in economic ideas across the entire political spectrum. The far-left politicians prove to be among the most assiduous readers and citers of economists of all the groups in this study, more attentive overall than the centre left. They tend to mention a mix of what many would describe as "heterodox" economists (see the Preface for a definition), and to stipulate that the *only* economists whose authority they respect are heterodox.

I interviewed politicians from Die Linke in Germany, British Greens and Corbynite Labour in the UK, the Red–Green Alliance and Alternativet in Denmark and the PCF in France. I did not interview anyone in the Democratic Party whose goals were of an equivalently radical level, so the US politicians are excluded from this section.

Far-left interviewees are radical in their economic thinking, explicitly identifying with socialist or "ecological-socialist" economic goals. For example, a British Green says, challenging materialism, "I've always thought the problem was people being encouraged to see themselves as producers and consumers rather than as spiritual beings." A British Corbynite adviser says the nature of the economy is that "there's a small group of people in charge who exploit everyone else and nature and this is how the economy works in a fundamental sense". Politicians on the far left readily articulate economic goals of "a new, fair economic order" (German Die Linke politician), and recognize that this might require quite thoroughgoing transformation, to "reallocate resources and change the way citizens are perceived, not as cogs in a capitalist machine but as individuals with intrinsic value" (British Green).

The far left has an approach of bracketing all neoclassical or mainstream economists together as mistaken, favouring heterodox economists only. Out of all groups, far-left interviewees use the terms "neoclassical" and "heterodox" most often. They reject neoclassical assumptions about economic actors being rational and self-interested. They reject neoclassical economists' claim to be "value-free" or "objective". As a Corbynite adviser says, "There is always a nub of economics that is about politics." A British Green politician describes neo-classical thinking as a "control system rather than an explanatory system". The Corbynite adviser, formally trained in mainstream ideas, agrees: "The neoclassical framework … the methodology of it, even the ontology of it is basically wrong. Methodological individualism is a wrong way to think about society."

Others just go straight to individual strands of thinking that would usually be classed as heterodox, such as "Marxism". In fact, some German and Danish centre-left interviewees also support Marxism as some kind of foundation. For instance, a German SPD politician says, "I would rather locate myself in a mixture of Marxist and Keynesian, so, in relation to my practical politics, it is Keynesian, because Marxist is an ideal for me; that is a vision." A Danish Social Democrat expresses views that would be anathema to most American Democrats when he says that, in the social democratic part of parliament that he belongs to, "Marx is practically taught with the mother's milk". He expounds that Marx is "foundational", but that Keynes belongs to how he "utilizes" the economy. Keynesian ideas have been proved to work and also to adapt to modern conditions. He does not agree with economists who say that the ideas of the two thinkers are incongruent: "If you understand how the productive forces determine what is available in society [as Marx teaches], then that materialization must benefit the future. I think Keynes has been a good lever for that."

If far-left politicians mention Keynesianism, they are explicit that they mean the "left" versions, which many economists would categorize as heterodox. Among far-left interviewees mentioning Marxism, a common tendency for Die Linke politicians is to say that they are Marxist and "left" Keynesian. Generally, the Die Linke politicians discuss economic ideas in quite productivist[3] terms, aiming for non-material change, in terms of areas such as ecology and feminism, but rooted in the classic economic goals of full employment and good work conditions. The way they talk about the need for Marx echoes how the centre-left colleagues who mention Marx talk about him, as providing an

---

3. "Productivist" in this context means believing that material standards for the working class need to rise and being sceptical of the de-growth stance of some ecological socialists.

understanding of power structures, although those on the far left embrace his thinking more fully.

The second group on the far left is less conventional and often more eclectic. The politicians in this group come from the British Greens and Corbynite left, the Danish far left and environmentalist parties such as the Red–Green Alliance and Alternativet. They are less conventional in the sense that they do not focus on Marx so exclusively, and many of the thinkers they mention are more recent, such as in the "post-Marxist" or ecological schools. A British left politician who spent years trying to persuade the more Marxist productivist far left to open up to decentralized environmentalist ideas describes them as "conventional" and having closed minds. A dominant feature of this eclectic second far-left group is that, rather than just plumping straight for one econo-mist, they usually start by explaining why they will listen to a wide range of economists, as long as they are not neoclassical.

Therefore, the eclectic far-left group reflects what many commentators (Lavoie 2006) characterize as the pluralist nature of heterodox economics, con-sisting of strands that are often complementary rather than rivals. A Danish Red–Green Alliance politician says he would consider himself "a Marxist or post-Marxist". He says he is not a "Communist", but believes class is a huge problem. His openness to both Marx and what many would argue is very dif-ferent post-Marxist thinking reflects the tendency for some in the eclectic group to talk about the need for an open mind. A French politician is on the border between far and centre left, but articulates well why politicians should not stick to one school. She says she draws on "institutionalists" such as John Kenneth Galbraith, but also post-Keynesians and ecological economists: "It is hard to belong to one school of thought only, and I find that, often, people who belong to only one school of thought make me feel tense because they are not open … It is a mix of all of that from which I pick bits here and there."

Two heterodox policies that some politicians raise are worth mentioning here. The first is modern monetary theory (MMT), with politicians some-times referencing the economist Stephanie Kelton. Modern monetary theo-rists say that countries, such as the UK and United States in this study, that issue and control their own currencies do not have to rely on taxes or borrow-ing when they want to spend, because they can print as much as they need as the monopoly issuers of the currency. Rising national debt should not be feared in the way that it is by many other economists. The second heterodox policy some politicians mention is universal basic income (UBI), which some call universal citizens' income. When a government adopts UBI it pays every adult citizen a set amount of income on a regular basis. This means the benefit system can be removed. People may still want to work, to earn more, but the guarantee of a minimum for all is seen by some as a solution to what is likely to be widespread unemployment in an automated "post-work" future. In both cases, the far-left politicians considering them are tentative and refer to reading pilot and applied studies. For example, on the need for a universal citizens' income, a British Green politician weighs up whether to adopt this radical policy, saying that we need "stronger communities and alternative sources of identity". People will no longer be able to find a sense of security through work because of automation, precarity and in-work poverty. She says: "So, instead, the state should provide everyone with a basic income and basic security." However, despite her commitment, she is also aware that a policy as radical as this needs to be tested, and she follows the various pilot schemes that have been conducted with great attention.

The left and calls for technocracy

How far do the left politicians respect the authority of economists? For both centre- and far-left politicians, "economists" in the generic sense do not seem to inspire respect in the sense that their technical expertise gives them authority. The politicians already know what their goals are. They mostly have not prioritized and do not prioritize in-depth reading of academic economics, even if long ago they studied it at university. Attachment to "Keynesianism" as an approach is useful because it helps them identify specific economists who might be on their wavelength about redistribution and so on. Attachment to other economists, such as those developing MMT, is useful when they are working on those specific policy areas. The more attentive far-left politicians are attached to economists, but often in a category that is fragmented, leading to positives because the strands of thinking can often be complementary, but negatives because they give the impression they are at an experimental and fluid stage.

However, this chapter illustrates that a major barrier to economic technocracy that is additional to the level of respect for economists is the increasing diversity of economic goals in politics. If we marry the continuing free-market goals of the right, which I explore in the following chapters, with the renewed strength of the far left, we have more diverse economic goals than at any time certainly since the start of the neoliberal era. With diversity tend to come contestation and resistance to technocrats' demands to take economic policy out of the political domain. Many centre- and far-left politicians opposed the attempts in the neoliberal era to "depoliticize" economic policy. I end this chapter with the far left's argument, echoed somewhat more faintly by the centre left, that economic policy-making *should* be contested.

A Die Linke politician says economic ideas should be the subject of "fierce debate". He explains, "I have always seen the economy as a contested – also politically contested – field, in which different social interests of different population groups meet." A French Socialist says, "But, in the economic domain, the exchange of ideas is absolutely crucial: confrontation. You have different schools, which will obviously lead to very different proposals." Depoliticization fuelled a sense among some lower-income voters that they had been locked out of economic decision-making, leading to populism. Another French Socialist describes depoliticization as having closed down public participation, with disastrous consequences: "Economic questions are always used to avoid having citizens claiming things, as a means for violence – symbolic violence."

Politicians on the left think depoliticizing and decontesting, trying to give the impression that everyone has the same economic goals and pandering to the narrow view of voters as inherently self-interested, as we have seen in Chapter 3, work to the advantage of the right. However, this French Socialist also reflects the views of some others on the centre and far left in thinking that, after decades of depoliticization, economic policy is becoming more contested again. The example she gives is the "gilets jaunes", or yellow vest protestors, who made the left realize they had to ally environmentalism with social justice. The yellow vest protests, which took place in France in autumn and winter 2018, and have continued intermittently since, were protests largely by working-class and lower middle-class voters, often in rural areas, who opposed fuel taxes and what they saw as rising economic inequality, encompassing disaffected voters from both left and right. The French Socialist politician says that, even though they were disruptive, and challenged the left, a benefit from them was that they raised the profile of economic issues. "We could again talk about fiscality. We could again talk about the wealthy and poor. All of this became much easier. In my opinion, more than the pandemic, it is this yellow vest crisis that allowed us to bring down the conventions in terms of the economy."

Conclusion

The left-wing interviewees sound increasingly confident. Some commentators argue that the confidence may not last beyond the temporary attachment to stimulus forced on governments by the pandemic. However, the pandemic is not as prominent a theme in these interviews as one would expect. The focus of left interviewees is on the twin crises of growing inequality, spurred by the 2008 financial crisis, and the environment, which I turn to in Chapter 8. They see "neoliberalism" as having been in retreat for some years. They do not think many new economists are emerging who might support the right. Instead, most of the new economic ideas, such as on monetary theory, are more suited to left-wing goals. If this chapter seems Europe-heavy, however, that reflects the sense from American Democrats of a more fragile confidence. They do not feel that they have the solid underpinning of commitments to welfare and redistribution to withstand a more long-term shift in economic ideas.

In an era in which economic goals are further apart than previously, economic policy is likely to be more politically contested than in recent decades, reducing both the desirability and viability of ceding more control to economists.

5

Denmark and Germany: "home-grown" economists

In Denmark we see that the Scandinavian model is what we all like, so, having an academic from the UK or the United States, it's difficult because people are looking at them saying: "Oh, do you really want to have that system, as they have in the United States?"

(Danish Liberal, former minister)

I can't ignore science. Politicians are not obliged to implement the advice of science, but they must know and listen to science. Afterwards, politicians alone can decide.

(German CDU/CSU politician)

In this chapter I consider the attitudes of Danish and German politicians towards economists. I consider them together, because they are often categorized as "coordinated" economies, both with consensual political systems. In the case of Denmark, I focus on the politicians from all parties to show how there is a consensus on economic ideas. There is also a commonality in how Danish politicians see economists that spans across the political spectrum. However, in the case of German interviewees, I have already considered left and far-left German interviewees in Chapter 4. The attitude of the German right to economists is distinct from that of the German left; therefore, in this chapter, the focus is on the German right alone.

One feature that ties the interviewees together in this chapter is a relatively high degree of respect for economists, but of the home-grown variety only. Denmark and Germany each have councils of economic advisers that are independent of government and check on the soundness of their economic policies.

The Danish councils[1] are chaired by four university economics professors, who are often referred to as the "wise men"; one interviewee even described them as "wizards", somewhat ironically. In Germany, two of the current members of the Council of Economic Experts are women, and they tend to be referred to as "the sages". I found similarities in the relatively high degree of respect Danish centrist and the German right interviewees showed for these home-grown economists' professional authority, whether "sage" or "wise". Technocrats might argue that this Danish and German respect for experts means that they do not need to cede power to them as, by definition, they must already be delivering "responsible" economic policies. However, in the German case in particular, economic policy is becoming more contested, and there has been some shaking of faith in economic expertise.

I analyse the Danish interviews first, followed by the German right.

Denmark: the Scandinavian welfare model

Danish politicians were the most curious of all five countries about why we had chosen their country for a five-country study. They were interested in whether they were perceived as classic "Scandinavian", to compare with more liberal market economies, or whether we had we chosen them for their size. The answer was: for both reasons. Danish interviewees were nearly always keen to stress how small their country is, with a population of just 5.8 million. It seems to be one factor that has always led them to support an open economy.[2] It is also the case that they have a Scandinavian welfare-based economic model, developed since the 1960s to provide generous entitlements to education, housing, health and social benefits.

Denmark has an impact on the world stage as a beacon for social democratic ideals. Economic inequality is lower in Denmark than in most OECD countries, 26.4 on the Gini coefficient scale, compared with the United States' 39.[3] Living standards are high; Denmark's GDP per head is on a par with the OECD's best performers.[4] Despite the large public sector, the Danish model is not straightforwardly a "planned" one in old-style socialist terms. The country

---

1. In addition to the Economic Council there is the Environmental Economic Council; both councils are chaired jointly by the four professors.
2. Denmark is a member of the European Union, although, unlike France and Germany, it is not a member of the eurozone. It has a high level of exports and imports and ranked 16 out of 207 countries on the KOF Globalisation Index for 2018 (see https://kof.ethz.ch/en/forecasts-and-indicators/indicators/kof-globalisation-index.html).
3. See https://data.oecd.org/inequality/income-inequality.htm.
4. See www.oecd.org/denmark-economic-snapshot.

has a thriving private sector based on financial services, which usually achieves high rates of growth. Denmark's infrastructure combines with a flexible labour market to contribute to it being seen as an attractive place for entrepreneurs: the World Bank ranks it fourth out of 190 countries for "ease of doing business" (World Bank 2020).

What do existing studies lead us to expect about how Danish politicians see economists? Three themes emerge. The first is that Danish economists have been less influenced by neoliberal ideas from the Anglosphere. Johan Christensen (2017), for example, in his study of the economists within the state bureaucracy, says that, compared with other small states, Danish economists had less contact with Anglosphere economists in the 1980s and 1990s. Denmark did not respond to the crises of the 1970s in the same way that countries such as France, the UK and the United States did, by a wholesale paradigmatic shift from Keynesian demand management to "neoliberalism" (see also Stahl 2022). Instead, Keynesianism remained dominant, and, somewhat later, Danish economists integrated some supply-side ideas into that framework. For example, Stahl says that, although Liberal Party politician Anders Fogh Rasmussen had been influenced by Chicago supply-side economist Robert Lucas in the 1980s, he had not been able to develop support for the new ideas to take a real hold on either economists or politicians by the time his government ended. John Campbell and Ove Pedersen (2014: ch. 7) compare economic research organizations, including the independent councils that advise national governments in Denmark, France, Germany and the United States. They confirm that the Danish council's reports were far less "neoliberal" throughout the period (from the 1980s until the 2008 financial crisis) than in the other three countries.

The second theme to emerge from existing studies is that Danish economists tend to agree with each other, to be less divided than in some other countries. Campbell and Pedersen (2014: ch. 7) report that there were few signs of the "flip-flopping" in the national council's advice that happened in the United States when Democrat administrations replaced Republican administrations, and vice versa. Instead, there was consistency in the economists' advice whether a "red" or "blue" coalition was in power. They say that this reflects the "general proclivity for negotiation and consensus making", which is "institutionalized". They describe Danish economists as a closely connected "brotherhood". The consensus view is "a taken-for-granted acceptance of the virtues of social democracy".

Third, on the whole, Danish economists are portrayed as having a low level of influence on economic policy. Christensen (2017) argues that, in comparison with Norway, Ireland and New Zealand, economists in the state bureaucracy in Denmark have a lower level of influence, somewhat fragmented between departments. There are not as many powerful economic think tanks in Denmark. The Danish state directs economics more, which implies a potentially higher level of politician influence. For example, it was Social Democrat politician Mogens Lykketoft, who had been trained as an economist, who spearheaded the integration of supply-side ideas into tax policy, ensuring that it stayed progressive and that a social democratic economic approach was sustained, by economists and politicians alike.

In interviews with Danish politicians in 2021, which economic ideas seem predominant and what do they say about the ideas of the economists who influence them? I started conducting the 17 Danish interviews in February 2021, having waited for the pandemic second wave death rate to decline. Most did the online interview in fluent English, and six spoke in Danish. There are a large number of small political parties in Denmark, which is nearly always ruled by a coalition, although at the time of the interviews there was a minority Social Democrat government led by Mette Frederiksen. I invited politicians from both the national parliament, the Folketing, and the European Parliament to talk to me. I chose politicians who had shown an interest in economic policy, by being a spokesperson or serving on an economic committee. Six of our interviewees had also served as ministers with economic portfolios. I selected interviewees from parties that represented "right to left" in terms of the overall position of each party.[5]

Danish politicians had quite business-like backdrops. If they were in their offices, they often sat in front of noticeboards or unadorned walls. A former minister had left politics a couple of years beforehand and worked in a corporate environment. He was one of the few to have expensive-looking artwork on the white-painted walls of his office. He did not need to be in the office, as during lockdown there was the option to work from home, but there were too many distractions there. He looked out of a bright open window to the side of his computer and was cheerful and engaged through the whole interview, thanking me whenever I asked an autobiographical question, because it was a luxury for him to reflect. The Danish interviewees were the youngest of the five countries. Some had got into politics early, achieved ministerial status and then left politics, not necessarily indicating that that was a final decision.

---

5. The interviewees were drawn from the following political parties: two were "far right", one each from the Danish People's Party and the New Right party; two were Conservative; one was Liberal Alliance, an economically liberal party; two were from the main Liberal Party (Venstre); one was a Social Liberal; four were from the dominant Social Democrat party; one was from occasional Social Democrat allies the Socialist People's Party (Socialistik Folkeparti: SF); and four were from "far-left" parties such as the Alternativet and the Red–Green Alliance.

Perhaps because of the size of the country or the consensus they describe, they gave the sense that the worlds of politics, trade unions, business and economics were intertwined.

"Responsible" economic policies: Danish consensus

Taking as a benchmark the position that economists tend to have a "value-free" approach, Danish politicians express beliefs about the need for welfare and security, in more normative terms. Their commitment to collective solidarity runs counter to the emphasis many neoclassical economists would put on efficiency or the selfish rationality of individuals and their need for financial incentives. One of the questions we asked interviewees was when they first became aware of the economy – in effect, their earliest memory. A Danish politician for the Social Democrat party describes her earliest economic memory. Her mother worked in a children's home. Her mother used to explain to her, from when she was very young, that "not every child is equally lucky or born into a good family". This was in the 1970s, when Denmark's Social Democrats were establishing what would become a classic Scandinavian welfare-based economy. Her mother told her that it was important that "we have a social democratic *society* that helps those children who aren't as lucky. That requires an *economy* that can help those children". She goes on to describe how, as an adult politician, she has played her part in developing and sustaining what she calls the "social democratic economic model". Many Danish politicians echo her belief that the purpose of the economy is "to help those children".

Economic policy-making is not an end in itself, to promote efficient markets and growth, but a "tool" for shaping society. Danish politicians tend to see the economy and economic policy-making as encompassing social issues, contrary to the separation of the economy from other human spheres underpinning the neoclassical economic canon. Listen to how two politicians define the term "economic" itself. A far-left politician says: "And I consider that you are talking about economics in the broad term, so all of these things – welfare and public goods – are of course economic policies". A Socialist People's Party former minister describes how his earliest political memories are about observing social differences, and says that, "obviously", economics is "part of that".

Politicians' support for both generous welfare and social equality is expressed in two ways. First, there is a dominant emphasis on the moral case for security. Discussing housing, the former SF minister says that both middle- and lower-income families need a "security blanket" guarantee of "decent" housing. Second, many politicians explicitly argue in favour of "equality" itself, not limited to the version of "equality of opportunity" favoured by their US counterparts. When the former minister talks about the value of a "more equal society", he means equal outcomes, which are necessary to promote genuine equality of opportunity: "The *more equal society* you have, the better prospects the society and children [have] to actually use their intellects to actually get a career, get an education and have a good life and actually have some hope about their further doings in life."

Politicians often contrast Denmark's greater equality of outcomes compared with the United States. The former minister was shocked by the poverty that existed alongside riches during a period in his teens when he lived in the United States. Even a young far-right adviser paints the "extremely unequal society" of the United States as bleak, where there is not "one society but 20". Only when he travelled did he realize how lucky he was to live among the "beautiful, peaceful, extremely rational and friendly people we have in [Denmark]", a different conceptualization of what "rational" means compared with the self-interested version of economics.

Most Danish politicians' moral commitment to the broader society is exemplified by their attitude to their (high) tax burden. The former SF minister again is enthusiastic about high taxation to a degree not expressed by a single American interviewee: "Even though I earn a bunch of money now, *I still pay my taxes with incredible happiness*, because I know they lay the bricks in our society, and it's so important."

However, the second string to how most of the interviewees talk about the economy is that, as well as seeing their social democratic model as morally desirable, they do also see it as economically viable – efficient, even. Although one might have expected that politicians from left-wing parties would be keen on welfare and a large public sector, they also support a relatively unregulated private sector. One Social Democrat, who sees himself as in the middle of his party, stresses support for the private sector by saying he believes in "as much market as possible, as much regulation as necessary". Many use the term "flexicurity" and express pride in it. "Flexicurity" is a combination of "security" from welfare and a "flexible" private sector, which leads to high rates of growth. Workers' security based on generous unemployment benefits makes trade unions more ready to agree to entrepreneurs firing workers. Entrepreneurs also have greater flexibility in hiring, because the welfare state means they can draw on educated workers with housing, health- and childcare support and a well-maintained infrastructure.

Most Danish politicians explicitly engage with economic ideas that equate efficiency with a small public sector. They see the large public sector as benefiting the private sector, not draining or crowding it out. An elder Social Democrat, and one of the architects of the mix of private sector and welfare economics, explains that "the [high] taxes were not a waste of money; it was an investment in education, it was in investment in women's participation, kindergartens, and so on; it was an investment in people actually being more mobile when they feel safe in going from one job to another". He says in the past "neoliberal economists" told them their large public sector would crowd out the private sector and their model would not allow them to "fly". But Denmark is like a "bumblebee" and has confounded expectations, leading to consistently high rates of growth.

The pandemic had increased Danish politicians' confidence in the economic viability of their system. Politicians' fears about the virus were as acute as in any of the other countries, but it did not seem to have shaken their underlying beliefs. Another Social Democrat MP says that the pandemic has confirmed for him how strong the Danish economy is in "innovation". He compares Denmark favourably with the nearest economic powerhouse, Germany: "We are far ahead on digital platforms relative to other countries; telefax is still commonly used in Germany. We are far ahead on the green agenda and far ahead on medical areas as well."

To his right, a Conservative chooses to stress that one of the reasons the Social Democrat government can borrow in the pandemic without "harming" the economy is because of past sustained fiscal responsibility and low debt, which he implies that he credits all centrist parties for. This fiscal responsibility is one factor that encourages Danes to pay for welfare through high taxation. Denmark has a "robust" base.

This belief in the robust and solid foundations is shared by his far-left counterpart, who chooses to focus on the parts of the foundations that are about welfare. He says the pandemic shows that countries with a strong social security system fare better. He believes this is leading to further retreat of the "neoliberal epoch's" beliefs in a minimal state.

Danish attitudes to economists

On the surface, Danish politicians demonstrate a high level of respect for economists' professional authority. On the whole they listen to what the "wise men" who chair the economic councils say. On a quantitative measure, they mention economic schools of thought and named economists more often than their American counterparts. Qualitative analysis of their interviews also confirms that they show one of the highest levels of respect for the professional authority of economists of any of the five countries, because when asked directly if they think economists are "useful" the vast majority, from all parties, give positive responses. For instance, a Social Democrat MP says that "[economists] are very important for our society. We need people who go into the big machine room and look at all the small screws one can twist and turn. I also think some of them sometimes take us down the wrong roads, which I could have done without. But, overall, they are useful." However, the respect is based on the fact that the economists they refer to share their ideas. They give the impression that they have moulded the economists over the years, rather than the other way around. As a former Social Democrat minister puts it, "Politicians have helped economists carve out a special role [in the policy-making process]." To understand the attitudes of the politicians towards economists, one has to start with the remarkable consensus in politics.

A Conservative says, "Social democracy dominates how politicians from all the centre parties think about the economy." He demonstrates how far he supports the welfare model, despite being a "Conservative", when he says that "we need to have some kind of control and regulation in order to make sure that we maintain values". A second Conservative says he does not believe in "the liberal case" that the state should have no influence. He says: "I am Conservative, so I believe that the state should still play a role. I believe in a free market, but the market needs to be *interpreted*." They echo the left's belief that the strong welfare state benefits the private sector: the first claims it is a "fact" that "a good public sector is important also to the private sector". He thinks that "three factors" encapsulate why the Danish economic model is successful: the second and third are the "flexible labour market and the management culture"; but his first factor is the "well organized society", which again demonstrates how broad the support for the welfare model is.

One illustration of the consensus is that Danish Social Democrats do not tend to proclaim themselves as "Keynesian" the way that social democrats do in other countries, as a kind of oppositional stance to market-conforming economics. They tend to say they are Keynesian in the sense that it is just the dominant backdrop economic good sense that prevails in their country. As a Liberal politician, formerly an economist, says, she was "brought up" with Keynes. Liberals and Conservatives share this sense of Keynesianism as common sense with the more left parties. They also recognize the importance of "supply-side" approaches and reinforce the view in existing literature on Denmark that economists and politicians integrate supply-side ideas into a Keynesian framework, rather than going in a "neoliberal" direction as the UK and United States did in the 1980s.

The centrist politicians describe what they see as a parallel consensus among Danish economists by stressing their support for "home-grown" Danish economists only, who tend to emerge from the two main universities, in Copenhagen and Aarhus. The former economist who is now a Liberal politician says her economics degree was broad-based and practical:

My economic studies at Copenhagen were less focused on the economic models and very much focused on learning about the institutions of society. We always said that people who had my education would be able to read the *Statistical Yearbook* and get a sense of proportions in society, the development of population and systems of wage development and unionization. What kind of traits do we have, what is the development of agriculture? So it was an education which was very broadly developing how you would see society.

A former Liberal minister is more critical of the welfare model than his more left-of-centre colleagues, but even he says that his ideas "have come from some of the very old-school Danish politicians slash economists". I have quoted him at the head of the chapter as describing how Danish politicians and voters tend to assume that foreign economists will have more of a US perspective, which they do not want to pay attention to because it might result in a society that is completely different from the Scandinavian model they want. He says that, if a non-Scandinavian economist such as Joseph Stiglitz or Thomas Piketty comes into the discussion, "it's more like a curiosity. They're saying something interesting, [but] no one is actually trying to take what they're proposing and implement them in today's politics." The significant point here is that the two economists he chooses, Stiglitz and Piketty, are associated with anti-neoliberal positions. Therefore, their irrelevance is not that they would not appreciate the welfare model that Danes prize but that they would not understand it well enough to be able to promote and develop it the way home-grown economists do.

Politicians think economists have worked seamlessly with them to generate a consensus on ideas and that they are embedded in a consensual policy-making process. A Social Democrat former minister says there is a high degree of consensus on "the fiscal rules and the way you approach long-term structural challenges. I think that's pretty unique for Denmark." He says this has been achieved through building "cross-party alliances" not just in politics but in all the state's institutions, including at the level of economists in the bureaucracy. He describes this economic policy-making consensus as "operational", involving a homogeneous network of economists and centrist politicians, many of whom studied alongside each other. Danish politicians do not make as many of the complaints about economists being too "abstract" or "theoretical" that other politicians in this study make. Instead, economists "are very, very directly involved and their input is used in an extremely practical manner in policy-making or reform preparation processes."

Are there any signs of the Danish consensus breaking down? A few politicians coming from the culturally and economically liberal Liberal Alliance and one of the far-right parties, the New Right,[6] are fervent followers of Anglosphere "liberal" economists. The Liberal Alliance passion for "economic liberalism" is manifest in one former youth wing supporter's account of meetings at which they were "popish" in their support for Hayek and Friedman, wearing their names on T-shirts. A far-right economic liberal is more inspired by Estonian than US economists, but he is the one interviewee to talk often about the need for personal economic freedom, in ways that echo some of the American interviewees. He works tirelessly to avoid entrenchment of what he describes as "basic hardcore socialism" and is "inspired" to change the "economic direction". But, compared with all the other countries in the study, most notably the United States and the UK, Danish economic liberals are very much a minority voice; they argue that the dominance of social democratic and Marxist ideas among key professions such as teaching shapes the ideas of the young and makes it hard for them to challenge those ways of thinking.

Germany

If a picture is emerging of Danish politicians, at least from the large centre, having a consensual approach to economic policy and a fair degree of respect for home-grown economists, who they know well, how far is this true of German politicians? Like Denmark, Germany is often characterized as a "coordinated" market economy – in fact, the epitome of it (Hall & Soskice 2001; Hall 2018). Campbell and Pedersen (2014: 130) see coordination as stemming from corporatism – "where the state depends on certain interest groups in civil society to help make sense of and solve the country's economic problems". Peter Hall (2018) describes coordinated market economies as drawing on traditions of high levels of coordination between the producer groups of employers and workers. The Germans have a tradition of "co-determination": worker representation on councils making decisions in firms about wage bargaining, conditions and training.

The leading economic power in Europe, German per capita GDP and productivity are among the highest in the OECD.[7] Their Gini coefficient of inequality is 28.9, close to Denmark's and much lower than the United States'.[8] The German economy depends on export of manufactured capital goods, which were hard hit by the decline in global trade during the pandemic. Germany

---

6. This party is distinct from the older Danish People's Party, which is also culturally far right but with a more changeable and less liberal economic stance.
7. See www.oecd.org/economy/germany-economic-snapshot.
8. See https://data.oecd.org/inequality/income-inequality.htm.

also faces environmental challenges. As a result of fossil fuel dependence and the large manufacturing sector, its per capita greenhouse gas emissions are higher than in France, the UK or Denmark. Germany had been making efforts to decarbonize, through emissions pricing in heating and transport, and encouraging electric vehicles and renewable energy, but there are concerns that the pandemic might derail some of these efforts.

The German approach to economic ideas has some distinctive features. Most scholars point to the dominant postwar school of thought of ordoliberalism as being more than a strand of economic thinking and closer to an ideology than, for example, Keynesianism. Scholars such as Kenneth Dyson (2017) and William Sorley (1926) call ordoliberalism a "tradition" rather than just an economic school of thought, because it does not rest on positivistic utilitarian foundations of pleasure for the maximum number but also on desirable social and political goals. Key "Freiburg school" economists such as Ludwig Erhard, who had monitored the pitfalls of hyperinflation during the inter-war Weimar Republic and the dangers of political and social instability, sought political positions to rebuild Germany after 1945. They drew on some "Austrian school" ideas from economists such as Hayek and von Mises and were committed to free markets and competition. However, they saw the market as less autonomous from the state than those more liberal schools. A dominant theme in the interviews is the perception of the state as setting the "framework conditions" that the market needs to thrive in. These framework conditions include the "social market" to guarantee some social harmony and a commitment to stability over time, through economic policies that are sustainable and long term.

I include politicians from three broadly right-wing parties in this chapter, having included politicians from the German left in Chapter 4. First, I include politicians from the centre-right CDU/CSU parties, who have been in power for much of the postwar period. As a large party, the CDU/CSU spans quite a range of economic views and interpretations of the "social market". Second, I include politicians from the FDP, because they prove to be pro-market in their economic ideas, even if some might categorize them to be "centrist" overall. Third, I include three politicians associated with the AfD. Only one is still a member. The other two were initially drawn to the AfD for economic policy reasons. They thought the CDU/CSU was weakening key ordoliberal tenets. They then left the AfD when it became overwhelmingly focused on an anti-immigrant agenda. Therefore, interviewees associated with the AfD do not tend to represent its newer anti- immigrant members. In common with the reluctance of Rassemblement National politicians from France to agree to talk to us, AfD politicians from the more far-right wings of the party also refused to talk to us.

From the existing literature, we would expect German politicians on the right to have a high degree of respect for the professional authority of economists. Campbell and Pedersen (2014: 18) document the high level of "expert commissions" set up by governments in the postwar period, to compensate "for the federal ministries' limited technocratic expertise by providing analysis and advice to policymakers". They describe Germany's "consensus-oriented" economic policy-making as being based not just on the coordination of producer groups but also on respect for expertise, which ensured that "the dialogue among these groups remained rational and objective" (2014: 18). Each major political party tends to have a significant and well-funded research organization to support economic expertise. The Council of Economic Experts consists of economists and is more independent from government than, for instance, the Council of Economic Advisers in the United States. Campbell and Pedersen analysed its reports, finding a high degree of technical expertise underlying them.

In their analysis of how far the national economic councils that exist in Germany, France and Denmark "converged" during the 1980s and 1990s in the "neoliberal" direction that US economists were taking, Campbell and Pedersen (2014: ch. 4) argue that German economists had always been predisposed to free markets. However, they strengthened this with some greater emphasis on supply-side measures in the 1980s, which may have reflected some "Anglo" neoliberal influence. Having done so, they then continued on a course of being quite consistent over time. Campbell and Pedersen also characterize the German economic knowledge regime as being less divided or pluralist than that in France. However, their analysis stops in 2007. Other commentators note, as is reflected in our interviews, that the "ordoliberal" orthodoxy has been challenged more in recent years. We have seen that this was true in the case of the German left in Chapter 4. But, as I go on to show, even politicians attached to ordoliberal economic thinking are uneasy about whether those ways of thinking are as relevant in what seem to be changed economic conditions from 2008 onwards.

"Responsible": ordoliberalism

German right-wingers sound more normative when they discuss their economic goals than, for example, British right-wingers. They speak about holding "economic values" that relate to the need to help the poor by having a social market of welfare alongside a free market. Some Danish and German centre-right politicians are keen to dissociate themselves from "economic liberal" values of free-market efficiency, in the sense that they have other goals such as stability and, in some cases, distributive justice. German right-wing politicians often preface their support for freedom with observations about the iniquities of planned economies in neighbouring eastern European countries before the fall of Communism. At the same time, they talk about the moral underpinning of their version of freedom, such as the first CDU/CSU politician: "Freedom has a lot to do with responsibility. Freedom to choose what you want, of course. But then rules also have to be adhered to." The rules he elaborates on in this context are connected with achieving the goal of social stability. To do this, they aim for economic growth, which, according to a current AfD politician, "creates the greatest benefit for all involved", and they believe that the state should ensure minimum standards of welfare for all. According to a former AfD politician, "The idea of the social market economy is that no one falls through the cracks, but that there is mutual give and take in order to keep the individual within society." Society must keep all individuals "included". However, these current and former AfD politicians are also critical that many in the CDU/CSU have stretched the original ordoliberal commitment to social stability too far in order to justify excessive welfare spending, which undermines the incentive to work. One CDU/CSU politician who agrees with them jokes that "it's quite hard to find [ordoliberals] any longer [laughs]. In fact, I know hardly any in my party, the CDU/CSU … The ideas of Ludwig Erhard, who once was the German chancellor from my party – they are neglected, they disregard it."

German right-wingers use the term "ordoliberal" to describe their economic ideas, often declaring: "I am an ordoliberal." One says that ordoliberalism is the second best system, echoing the dictum that nobody has yet found the best. They are more consistent than other groups in respecting *one* economic school. For instance, Danish politicians have a high level of respect for "Danish" or "Scandinavian" economic schools, but intermixed with support for "Keynesianism". The British and American right tend to describe themselves as "free marketeers" rather than naming a school. French right-wingers do more often describe themselves as "economic liberals", but not all of them do, and, in any event, this is arguably a vaguer term than "ordoliberal". The German right refers to the "principles" and "rules" of ordoliberalism as if it is a school that prescribes specific actions to a greater extent than other right-wing politicians who use the "liberal" descriptor. The way German right-wingers often talk about ordoliberalism as a "system" indicates both how it prescribes policy in a number of areas, from the avoidance of debt to strict anti-monopoly laws and maintenance of a social market, and how, practically, it has guided much German economic policy over the postwar period. The current AfD politician gives a sense of the contribution of economists at a key point in the country's national history when he says that, "if we understand ordoliberalism correctly (of course, many do not understand it, so you have to explain it clearly), then, of course, that is the teaching that was embodied by the Freiburg school and many big names that we also know. Ludwig Erhard, Alfred Müller-Armack and Wilhelm Röpke are among them and many others after the Second World War."

A key feature of the appeal of ordoliberalism is commitment to sustainability and justice between the generations. German politicians see the long-term perspective of ordoliberalism as inherently "responsible" in this respect. They advocate "sustainable" finance. For instance, they tend to be debt-averse, proactively supporting the "black zero".[9] They argue that states should save in good times in order to be able to spend in emergencies, such as the 2008 financial crisis, which was rightly followed by a period of attempting to get finances back into balance. None are overtly critical of German domestic constraint or the leadership role Germany played in promoting austerity in relation to southern EU members such as Greece, even if a few think the tone could have been more diplomatic or the rationale better explained. They are highly troubled by pandemic-induced debt. They see spending as necessary but want it to be over as soon as possible, to get back to normal. One who thinks that current spending is going too far says: "Nobody really cares about paying those debts back, which means only two things: either that our children and grandchildren have to pay it back or we are running into a huge inflation, which is the payback automatically." For most, it is clear that unchecked debt will lead to further economic problems, such as inflation. Economic "laws" are like "gravity", which politicians ignore at their peril. For example, a German right-wing politician points to the perceived dangers of lacking attention to constraining "principles":

> In this respect, politics failed because they thought … politics could ignore the fundamental rules and laws of the economy – and that just doesn't work. You can't build a system, you can't build an order, that neglects economic principles. Nobody in politics can do that … We know that the water always runs downhill, and you have to orient your policy accordingly.

Many say that in recent years they have incorporated actions to help prevent or mitigate climate change into their beliefs about what sustainable economic policy should encompass. The ordoliberals seem to see the economy as a highly naturalized entity with its own inherent inevitable dynamics, even as they talk

---

9. A commitment to rigidly balanced budgets.

about the "framework conditions" set by the state. But, even though they think that promoting environmental sustainability is the right thing to do, they are concerned that the conventional commitment to financial sustainability might lapse. A former AfD politician says:

> While everybody now knows, every business leader, every politician, believes and agrees, we must have sustainable policy vis-à-vis the environment, the same politicians violate this principle in other aspects, like, for instance, sustainable financial policies. You know, right now we are spending billions and billions of euros and don't care ... due, for instance, to the corona crisis ... They plunder, really plunder, the state finances, and very often also the social systems. There's hardly a system and country in the world where the health system is sustainable or where the pension scheme is sustainable. They all spend the money without regard to sustainability at the expense of the future – something they don't do anymore, or don't want to do anymore, on the environment.

As the dominant economic power within the European Union and eurozone, I expected the EU dimension to economic issues to be at the forefront of politicians' minds in Germany. I deliberately did not ask direct questions about their economic ideas in relation to the European Union, in order to gauge how far to the forefront of their minds it was. Overall, German interviewees talked less about the EU dimension than their French counterparts. Of the German interviewees, the former AfD members were the most concerned about the dilution of German ordoliberal principles as a result of the national government committing itself too much to the eurozone, which they saw as having become too ambitious to produce effective economic policies. However, the CDU/CSU members tended to be almost exclusively preoccupied with the two national challenges of decarbonization and maintaining competitiveness through digitalization and other innovation. This national perspective also dominated how they saw voters, as putting pressure on them largely for what they could achieve at the national level, rather than for their stances on European-level issues.

Respect for ordoliberal economists

Like the Danish centrists, German right-wingers are more enthusiastic than many other politicians in this study in responding to the direct question about whether they think academic economists are useful to them by accepting that they are useful and acknowledging their expertise. For instance, a CDU/CSU politician says:

> I'll say that in the political decision-making process ... one cannot do without advice and without the models of science. So, for every important question [in parliament], we said we needed an opinion on the important economic models. Without that, you can no longer make politics today, because the interactions have become so great that you really need institutes that deal in depth with the various scenarios. So, for me, the judgement of the major economic institutes, especially the Kiel Institute for the World Economy, but also others, was necessary, and I believe that is the case with almost everyone.

They do not raise any criticism of economists as being "divided" as much as other groups. On the other hand, that may be because they only interpret "academic" economists as referring to a narrow range of "ordoliberal" economists. This group often names economists during the course of the interviews. Almost all the names they cite are closely associated with ordoliberalism, the Freiberg school in particular. The only "outsiders" they consider respecting are close to the free-market ideas of the ordoliberals (Hayek, von Mises, Adam Smith), and they select explicitly within the ideas of those economists, in comparison to their wholesale support for ordoliberalism. The bodies they cite, such as the Council of Economic Experts, have – at least until recently – tended to reflect the ordoliberal orthodoxy. One says that "it is made up of the best economists in Germany" and should be listened to "even though its recipes are not always popular". They make it clear that they doubt the wisdom of Keynesian counter-cyclical borrowing, some saying they will listen to neoclassical economists "as long as they are not Keynes-based". One CDU/CSU politician says:

> Keynesianism, if it works, it's fine, but if it doesn't, and the state spends too much money on it, sets the incentives at the wrong time ... I believe that nowadays it is more and more difficult to set these mechanisms in motion, as you can see in the [pandemic] rescue programmes and their effectiveness. We don't know that all the money that is pumped into the market in the end also brings the [desired] effect or whether it was just a flash in the pan in the end.

Despite appearing more respectful of the "scientific" authority of economists than of most other groups, they have lost respect for economists since the 2008 crisis because they have come to doubt that economists have answers to what appear to be the new and puzzling conditions of secular stagnation in the post-2008 era.

An FDP politician says, "In the beginning I was convinced that [economists] are not just useful but they are necessary. I change my belief there a little bit." They are disconcerted that real-life economies have not been "obeying" the ordoliberal "laws", such as excessive debt leading to inflation. The FDP politician asks, "How is this possible?" But he notes that "*the economists* have not been able to develop new theories that explain the situation". He means the economists they trust, the ordoliberals on the expert council of state. In the FDP politician's case, he believes that economists need to branch out into areas, such as behavioural economics and applied economics, that take account of realities on the ground rather than forecasting. He thinks forecasting is useful, "but it's only a rough guideline". He would not "want to build anything on economic theory as such, because there are too many other factors that have to be taken into account".

Responsiveness

The curious point about German right-wing interviewees is that they claim to recognize and support economists who epitomize the German state in the postwar period, but they believe that they are swimming against the tide of public opinion. In some ways they talk like outsiders, but they are, to all intents and purposes, part of the dominant "establishment". They characterize the voters as mostly "anti-market", too much in favour of welfare spending, brainwashed by teachers who have leftist views. In this respect, they echo Danish and French liberal "outsiders". One German CDU/CSU politician says, "One of the hardest jobs I had as a politician was to get my ideas across and tell people that having a hard stance on tax cuts, having a hard stance on social welfare, does not necessarily mean I'm a hard-hearted person." The problem arises because other politicians promise voters excessive "gifts". A second CDU/CSU politician says: "The population, of course, basically loves people who say they will get more child support … You have to be careful; it is not always sensible to advocate sound economic policy."

Nevertheless, this second CDU/CSU politician does think there is a "part" of the population that understand his message. And German leftist politicians make similar complaints about voters in the opposite direction, arguing that, for instance, commitment to the "black zero" is deeply entrenched and that it is too easy for right-wingers to invoke fears of inflation to quash state spending on investment. Some German right-wingers are nevertheless sufficiently concerned about what they see as a lack of voter understanding of their economic perspective that they advocate for more voter education, and even attempt lectures to that effect themselves. I return to the subject of whether and how politicians attempt to "educate" in Chapter 9.

Despite these criticisms of voters, German right-wingers do not raise excessive anxiety about their ability to deliver what they see as "responsible" economic policies. They admit to having made some compromises at the EU level, to having been too "profligate" under the Merkel coalitions and to having been too reckless in pandemic spending. Since I finished interviewing, an SPD/Green/FDP coalition has taken power, confirming their fear that they might be out of step with that profligate voter mood. However, despite this, the German right is more confident in the plausibility and future viability of its economic ideas than its right-wing counterparts in either France or Denmark.

Conclusion: the most respectful towards economists

Much of the existing literature that treats ordoliberalism as distinctive and German politicians as respectful of economists' authority is borne out by these interviews. Technocrats might argue that German politicians do not need to give more power to experts because they already listen to them enough. Partly because of the aim for stability built into ordoliberalism from the start, they do aim for "responsible" economic policies in the sense that they claim to deliver for the long term. Either they are less derailed by what some describe as voter short-termism or their voters put less short-termist pressures on them. Whichever the case, they correspond more closely to representatives who seem capable of delivering responsible economic policies.

The same could be said of the consensual Danish centrists, with interpretations of the need for long-term planning in environmental policy well developed, as I show in Chapter 8. Nevertheless, in Denmark any assessment of economic experts as already in charge would be a simplification. In Denmark it seems to be the politicians who drive the consensus rather than economists, who are in second place. In Germany, although respect for economic authority still seems higher than in the other three European countries in this study, there is less of a consensus between left and right economic ideas, and economic policy is more contested than it is in Denmark. German ordoliberals are uneasy. Economics has become divided, with a Keynesian-supporting left. And, since 2008, these left-wingers have not felt as confident about "their" economists as they once did. Economic policy-making in this larger country, beset by almost insurmountable economic problems, makes it unlikely that German politicians will give up any additional power, as they are forced to engage more vigorously with voters about the costs and benefits of different solutions.

6

France: pluralist economics and populist threat

> Economists are very useful [to politicians]. They obviously have to be vulgarized – that is to say, made comprehensible to people ... But I think they help us. To be a good politician, you don't want to burrow too deeply into a subject – because, in that case, you become an expert, if you dig. Transferring underground, you'll never reappear on the surface.
> (Centre-right politician)

> I think that what is expressed in France through yellow vests etc. is frustration more than anger, and frustration that is linked to the feeling that, no matter the political changes, my daily life never changes.
> (La République en Marche politician)

In this chapter French politicians describe a cultural and institutional landscape that sets France apart from the coordinated and liberal market economy models of the other four countries in this study. Although I have discussed some aspects of French left ideas in Chapter 4, I bring other aspects of what French leftist politicians say in here so as to help us understand the perspectives of centrist and right-wing politicians and overall trends in the French approach. How do French politicians from the full range of parties interpret what "responsible" economic policies are and what the balance should be between being responsible and being responsive to voters? How do they see the role of economic experts? In line with politicians from the other four countries, I show that, despite being aware of great economic challenges, French politicians do not think it is necessary or desirable to cede more control to independent economic experts.

There is a huge body of scholarship on France's historic and distinctive pro-state-planning or "dirigiste" approach to economic policy-making.

Many have debated how far France went in a more "neoliberal" direction in the early 1980s and how its neoliberal turn might have been different from that in the UK and United States. Ben Clift (2016) shows how in the "thirty glorious years" after the war there was a common education for top civil servants and politicians, to some degree separate from academic economics, sharing an underpinning belief in the value of dirigisme. In those years France's dirigisme seemed successful, and was even copied by other countries. However, some critics, such as Jack Hayward (1986) and Michael Loriaux (1999), have argued that there were inbuilt inflationary pressures and a tendency for the state to be captured by powerful interests, leading to, for instance, an inefficient industrial policy by the 1980s. Unlike the governments headed by Thatcher in the UK, the Socialist president François Mitterrand (in power from 1981 to 1995) responded to the economic problems of the 1970s by launching a break with capitalism – in effect, a reinvigorated dirigisme, with nationalizations. However, by 1983 the economy was in a deep crisis, leading to a balance of trade crisis and capital flight, and Mitterrand took a more neoliberal direction.

Some see the French neoliberal turn as eroding French exceptionalism (Hall 2006). Clift (2016) argues that, by 2016, France has become "post-dirigiste". Even though it is still ruled by a small elite tending to come from a small group of leading universities, they have adapted, particularly because dirigisme is hard to maintain in the face of pressures stemming from globalization and full EU membership. Nevertheless, Clift says that France is still more highly regulated than some other EU countries. Therefore, on the one hand, France does not have the coordinated tradition and consensual political institutions of Germany and Denmark, but, on the other hand, it is still distinct from the less regulated and more liberal Anglosphere.

I find that politicians address this central point, about how dirigiste or post-dirigiste France has become, and are divided in how far they want the state to have a role. The importance of this theme for our central question about whether France should or could become more "technocratic", in order to meet the increasingly complex future pressures, is that – in common with the other four countries – French politicians *diverge* in what they see as "responsible" economic goals. This divergence and contestation of economic ideas would make it hard for French politicians to agree on which economic experts to consult. But I show that French politicians' attitudes to economists are surprising. We might have expected German or Danish politicians to pay a great deal of attention to their "home-grown" economists, or for the Anglosphere politicians to be in thrall to economists who scholars such as Marion Fourcade (2009) have always described as the most powerful and influential. However, in some ways it is French politicians in this study who pay the closest attention to economists of all. There is a paradox, in that they both contest economic ideas and accept the pluralism of economics in ways that other politicians do not manage to do.

French politicians' attitudes may be shaped by their economic context and what many claim is deep-rooted economic pessimism. I show that French politicians seem more anxious than others, beset by economic pressures and the overlapping waves of recent crises. French GDP per capita is 18 per cent below that of the best OECD performers, and of the five countries in our study it has the highest unemployment rates and one of the lowest productivity rates.[1] But, given some of the relative economic positives – more equality, for instance, than in the UK and United States, and less of a decarbonizing challenge than in Germany – the pessimism may relate also to how fearful French politicians are of populist parties winning elections and protesting, as in the yellow vests wave.

This cohort of interviewees includes six with significant ministerial experience as well as leading economic policy-makers in opposition parties. But there is some patchiness in which parties they come from. French political parties are numerous and have splintered and re-formed in recent years. These interviews represent the centrists well. Starting with the centre right, I secured interviews with eight prominent politicians from the current Les Républicains (with past allegiances to the Union for French Democracy or Union for a Popular Movement). I interviewed three from the governing La République en Marche party, key politicians at the heart of economic policy-making. I interviewed six Socialist Party (Parti socialiste: PS) politicians. Three more could be described as from the "far left": one current Communist, one environmentalist/socialist MEP and one adviser who came more from the environmentalist trade union side. However, I could not secure an interview with a politician from the left-wing La France insoumise. And I managed to secure only one interview with a politician associated with the far-right Rassemblement National, no longer a member of parliament. Despite strenuous efforts, I could not find any current RN members who would agree to talk to me about their economic ideas.

French politicians raise the European Union more than politicians from any other country. One reason many interviewees raise the European Union as an issue is because they see its economic approach as dominated by German ordo-liberalism. On the whole, French politicians were far less exercised about high levels of debt, including in the pandemic, than their counterparts in Denmark and Germany. They thought the European Union's austerity response after the 2008 financial crisis had been damaging. As a Socialist politician says,

---

1. See www.oecd.org/france-economic-snapshot.

"Thinking only in terms of rules [is] the whole story of the euro." An LREM politician thinks that, at the EU level, the Germans insisted on "tightening up policy too soon" following the 2008 crisis and that they have learned not to do this in their response to the pandemic. Nevertheless, he is also committed to how some of the challenges facing France have to be dealt with at the EU level: "The global taxation of big companies, the environmental tax at the global level, or at least at the European one – it is all the challenges of global regulations without global governance." But, for some interviewees, the reason to raise the issue of Germany is to make a comparison in national economic performance and culture. A French right-winger says that the German government "is more reactive; they are much more pragmatic".

Diverging ideas about what "responsible" economic ideas are

As with the other four countries, French politicians have a range of economic goals. If there was a convergence during the neoliberal era, there is less sign of that now. Clift (2016: 516) claims that economic ideas are "conspicuously conflictual" in France, which implies that, as well as being diverse, French politicians also contest economic policy. In this section I start with the economic ideas on the left and move through to the right.

The left

French interviewees see the divergence of ideas and how hotly they are contested as waxing and waning over time. They refer to "grand theory", by which they mean Marxism and Communism, as having been more dominant in the past. The neoliberal era crushed such thinking. A Communist politician describes this process. He says there was "a very important, pluralist and effervescent economic academic and political economic debate in the 1960s and 1970s". But in the neoliberal era "there was such ideological domination that the debate was extinguished, with those who didn't think that way having a hard time making themselves heard in the academic world". He describes the neoliberal era as not just having stifled the original Marxist and other leftist thinking but also stifling the potential for any new ideas to emerge. However, in the last ten years, thanks to a growing recognition of the dangers of inequality and the need to mitigate climate change, the situation has changed. In common with other left-wing interviewees, the Communist politician thinks ideas have "widened" in the last decade or so; he says that there is "now, again, a great excitement to think differently".

Where do French far-left politicians look for ideas? Like far-left politicians in the UK, French far-left politicians show that they pay attention to "hetero-dox" economists, from outside the neoclassical mainstream, on how to meet the new challenges. For the Communist politician, these are mainly schools of Marxist economics. He still wants to "rebuild industrial sovereignty" and re-establish public control over monetary and financial policies after a damaging era of deregulation. But he acknowledges that "the public services that we need to build today are not exactly the same as those that existed in the 1970s". Drives to restructure economic policy should no longer be material, based on growth. Instead, the drivers of economic policy should be "the preservation and the promotion of common goods" of social equality and protection of the planet. He is "very satisfied" that the notion of the common good "is coming back in public and economic debates". There is less of the emphasis on short-term profits of the neoliberal era. The radicalism of his economic ideas is clear, because he believes that "we need to completely reverse the logic" and develop "a post-capitalist economy". This requires "Marxism", but there are many debates within the Marxist strands of thought. It is a good thing that this debate is "opening up". However, in common with far-left politicians in the other countries, the French far-left interviewees all imply they are in a state of flux about which detailed policy paths to follow.

How confident do French left-wing politicians sound about the reach of their economic ideas? The fact that there has been a widening and opening up of ideas in the last decade or so does not mean that the days of "grand left theories" have returned. Far-left politicians, and to a lesser extent their centre-left colleagues, are less confident that their ideas will prevail than their counterparts in the other three European countries. An environmentalist socialist who could be described as to the left of the Socialist Party says one reason she lacks confidence is that France still has a "real problem with social dialogue" and "the building of policies". France still "very quickly" has strikes and people protesting out on the streets, but the structures of a high degree of trade union membership and traditions of involving workers in coordinated decision-making are not as present as they are in Germany and Denmark.

Centre-left interviewees do not express their ideas as normatively or emotionally as the Germans or Danes. They mention the need to "redistribute" to reduce inequality. For instance, one Socialist says: "So, I was elected as a Socialist so I have always thought that the questions of redistribution and the sharing of wealth were important; that social and environmental standards were also obviously important. So, it's these; these are the fields of action and the sectors in which you must always hold firm." A PS former minister says that "solidarity" is not just a social goal but "fundamental" to the functioning of "a good economy". His commitment to solidarity means he "avoids increases in inequality" and makes sure people are able to "progress". But he goes on to say that Socialists do not dwell on why redistribution is needed or elaborate on the desired extent of equality – for instance, whether of opportunity or outcome.

Centre-left interviewees also often describe themselves as "pragmatic" rather than "ideological". Some explicitly identify with what they describe as more moderate, "more German-style", "social democracy". The Socialist Party former minister says there was a debate for a long time within his party between "first left", which was more "statist and nationalizing", and "second left", which was more oriented towards "liberty and production". He was in the "second left" group, which, he argues, was also the only viable path following the 1983 neoliberal turn. He has always respected "the core values" that he thinks are intrinsic to the left, but he has an "extremely pragmatic vision" of what the state should do. His line has echoes in what a second former minister says, who describes believing in a balanced "form of economic management, of a mixed economy", and "reasonable growth ... a bit managed, a bit controlled, avoiding waste". Many centre-left interviewees are quick to define their economic ideas as "Keynesian". Similarly to some of their counterparts from the other countries, they do not go into much detail, but indicate that Keynesianism gives them a broad basis from which to intervene in the economy and achieve their redistributive goals.

The right

I explore how the centre-right politicians talk about their economic ideas, to establish how "liberal" they are. I argue that there is a divide in the centre-right interviewees between an enthusiastic economic liberalism, on the one hand, and a more statist approach, on the other.

First the "economic liberal" centre right. These politicians say they have an uphill struggle promoting their economic liberalism because it is so alien to the dirigisme of the French political system. In this sense they sound like outsiders, similar to the Danish economic liberal minority in Chapter 5. One who has been an economic liberal all his political life says liberalism is "not the French approach ... France is quite an astonishing country, in which there are practically no liberals ... The free marketeer – that doesn't exist." He explains that intellectuals are mostly leftist, having stayed "quite Marxist". French economist Thomas Piketty epitomizes the "large number" of economists in France who think capitalism is "abominable" and pursue nationalization. He struggled with his own rightist colleagues, who are too "Gaullist" in the statist tradition of Colbert:[2] "For the French right, there is nothing effective, nothing important, which isn't initiated by the state." He does think things are changing now, with a "new generation" of economists at least, but politicians and voters show themselves in the current pandemic crisis to still instinctively look to the state – "and that is why there are no liberals in France. The politician who says that it's thanks to business, the politician who, like Ronald Reagan, says "The state is not the solution, the state is the problem" in France – that would be an impossible revolution. But we need to hear that in France."

His colleague defines his version of "pragmatism" as entailing "adapting regulation to the needs of the economy and responding closely to the needs of companies". But the way he sees French politics is that you are either an economic liberal, as he is, believing in "freedom of enterprise, freedom to innovate, freedom to sell, freedom to export, freedom to import", or you "go back" to interventionism and dirigisme. These centre-right politicians stick with a "support for free markets because they are efficient" line, without as much talk of "values". For instance, the one just cited says he is convinced that entrepreneurial freedom and free-market competition is "the best model", implying efficiency. The centre-right politicians are more likely than those on the left to refer to the economy as an autonomous sphere and the possibility that one might have to adhere to its "rules".

The second group on the centre right, although they sometimes use the term "economic liberal", are more equivocal, or they also show strong support for policies to promote equal opportunities and stability. For instance, one former minister claims that "stability" and "equality of opportunity" are important and fundamental in a democracy. He defines equality of opportunity as meaning that one has "to allow a child, whatever social class they are born in, to go further, faster, higher". He accepts that politicians vary in how they interpret which social policies are necessary to achieve that goal. In his view, equality of opportunity requires education policies and "social policies of redistribution", among others. He describes himself as a "liberal in economic terms" because the private sector "creates wealth"; but he sees promoting wealth as requiring regulation that is "sufficiently powerful to avoid drama" while being "sufficiently discreet … not to hamper creation and productivity". A third former minister describes being "liberal right" (rather than economically liberal), which he defines as "entrepreneurial freedom, freedom of initiative, believing in innovation and in research progress" but also "state

---

2. Jean-Baptiste Colbert was controller general of finances in the late seventeenth century under King Louis XIV, and was credited with inaugurating a predisposition in France to believe that the economy should serve the state.

intervention". The problem is that, in France as well as on the left, "we also have people on the right who are big spenders". That politician's priority is to reduce waste and administration and increase flexibility to adapt tax regimes, including lowering taxes. The members of this second group, although they may support some economic liberalism, seem more in a European tradition in view of their emphasis on the state and social stability than the first, more Anglo-liberal group.

La République en Marche

It is illuminating how French interviewees from outside LREM view Macron's party, which was formed from scratch to fight the 2017 elections. In the run-up to the 2017 general election the key requirement for LREM candidates was to be determined to break the impasse of governments lurching from left to right and to bring expertise to bear on modernizing France, including prioritizing its economic development. Four years on, the question I asked is: do the other politicians believe LREM politicians have moved beyond "ideology" in their economic approach? Left-wing politicians claim that Macron has pursued an avowedly right-wing economic agenda. One Socialist who watched her young contemporaries join his party argues she was right not to, because his income tax reforms and "drastic" reductions in higher-rate taxation have been regressive, his reform of housing tax has been centralizing and he has opposed a minimum wage for young people. An adviser, working with trade unions on the green transition, says Macron has been tainted by his education in the United States, which has led him to pursue what he sees as right-wing economic policies that have provoked "the biggest social movements" since May 1968, in the form of the yellow vests.

Some on the right agree that LREM has been rightist in its economic direction, in the sense of economically liberal. A Les Républicains politician accuses Macron of having tried to merge centrists into a "big Macron casserole", but says Macron is nevertheless "obviously a liberal … certainly more liberal than me".

What of the LREM interviewees themselves? One describes having become "less liberal" since the 2017 election, more aware of how much the state already does and should continue to do. A second one describes himself as not having a detailed economic stance, but being predisposed to "believe in the market", while acknowledging its weaknesses and the role the state should play in correcting them. A third says he has always been sympathetic to the "British or Anglo-Saxon vision … that is to say that the economy has a function in itself and the state comes in to fulfil certain objectives or to do some changes, to frame things and to fulfil public policies". He says the problem with the French approach is that the state is seen as "pre-dating the economy and as creating the economy to serve society". Being in French politics, he has had to learn to tone down his Anglo-Saxon orientation.

Although some may argue that Macron's government started out "technocratic", I dispute this characterization. In countries where it is constitutionally possible to catapult in experts to become ministers, without them having to be elected, it may be meaningful to talk about "technocratic governments". But in France Macron and the LREM candidates had to stand for election. Four years on, they describe the pressures of being elected representatives, balancing responding to voters with the need to deliver responsible policies, just like those from other parties. The bigger question about "technocracy", and the main one I address throughout this book, is whether French politicians think they should go in the technocratic direction of ceding more power to "experts" who stay out of elected office. Despite all the problems they say they encounter, with protest and "immobilisme", none of the politicians call for a greater ceding of power to experts.

Contestation

The diversity and contestation of economic ideas does not seem greater than in the other four countries. But neither does it seem to be less. One LREM politician believes that "the economic culture in France is less developed" than in the Anglosphere: "There is a relation to the economy that is a little bit complicated in France." His Socialist colleague confirms his belief that many French leftist politicians think economic ideas should be contested when he says that, "in the economic domain, the exchange of ideas is absolutely crucial: confrontation. You have different schools, which will obviously lead to very different proposals." The politician who had been associated with the Rassemblement National was opposed to surrendering to the exigencies of globalization and supranational institutions, wanting to reclaim national sovereignty. He wanted to promulgate a new economic philosophy of "economic patriotism". This politician saw the main divide in politics as between "globalists" and "patriots": "Some defend the nation and the nation's interest, and then there are those who don't care about France and who are only looking to make a profit internationally and globally with the free movement across borders."

This reminder of the gulf in economic ideas between "economic patriotism", on the one hand, from a party that achieved a substantial proportion of electoral support, and economic liberalism and new forms of Communism, on the other, shows how diverse French politicians' economic goals are.

But recall that this is similar to the pattern in other countries. In Britain we had a heterodox left committed to universal basic income and a Eurosceptic right in the form of UKIP, willing to sacrifice international economic opportunities for sovereign gains; in Germany Die Linke draws on Marxist ideas for workers' rights and restructuring capitalism while the most right-wing ordoliberals still live by the "black zero" and minimal interpretation of what the social market should entail.

Attitudes to economists

Given the diversity, what attitudes towards economists do French politicians have? Do they respect their authority, and/or see them as providing any kind of unified consensus view? The leading economic sociologist of economists, Marion Fourcade (2009: 11), says the long-standing French tradition in economics is again affected by dirigisme: "The French economics profession derives its characteristics from a national political culture and institutional makeup centred on the administrative exercise of public power." French economists could be employed by the state, in which case they would become "technicians" involved in planning and implementation. Alternatively, if they stayed at a more theoretical level in universities, they would have less influence than, for example, their American counterparts, more frequently consulted by politicians.

But scholars of broader economic knowledge regimes, such as John Campbell and Ove Pedersen (2014), conducting their empirical research in the same period as Fourcade (2009) leading up to the 2008 financial crisis, come to different conclusions. They studied the French national economic council, called until 2008 the Conseil économique et social. The French council's annual reports exhibited a more open-minded and eclectic approach than those of the equivalent US and German councils in consciously drawing on university-based economists from a wide variety of schools. Campbell and Pedersen say that the French economists working in the state as "technicians" do rely on this external university-based advice. Agreeing here with Campbell and Pedersen, I find some politicians, perhaps more on the centre and right, showing a higher degree of attentiveness to academic economists than one might have expected from Fourcade's account. In some ways French politicians pay greater attention to academic economists than politicians in any of the other four countries.

In answer to my direct question "How useful do you find academic economists?", French politicians' responses are as positive as those of the German right and the Danish centrists. A far-left politician gives a typical response when he says that "we cannot have good economic policies as political actors without drawing sustenance from this research". But, before exploring the positivity, a minority have some criticisms. One criticism from a couple is that the whole discipline has become too "politicized". An LREM politician finds that, when she needs to rely on "economic theory or current economists to make an enlightened decision", she cannot find "objective data". Economists such as Thomas Piketty and Jean Tirole are too closely associated with political positions, and she is forced to depend instead on institutions that produce statistics rather than academic economists. She is also in a minority in complaining that economists do not have convincing answers as to why there have been economic conditions of secular stagnation for so many years, which many politicians voice in the other countries. On monetary policy she has "the impression that [economists] are just repeating things without more economic basis, ultimately, because everyone is very lost". Finally, again, even though the majority of politicians in other countries do this, this LREM politician is one of relatively few French politicians to criticize the abstraction of economists, how their research is not applied enough to be of use.

The big contrast between French centre- and far-left politicians and their British and, to a lesser extent, Danish and German counterparts is that the French do not rail as much against the dominance of the assumptions of rationality and self-interest that underpin the neoclassical synthesis. There is none of the need to itemize why they will listen only to "heterodox" economists, or even much use of the term "heterodox". This suggests that French economics has always been more plural, allowing perhaps for the maintenance of high-profile thinkers from traditions such as Marxism or ecology during the neoliberal era, and less hegemonic neoliberal thought.

The French politicians may be positive about the usefulness of economists, but their reasons are different from those of the Danish centrists and German right. The dominant view from French interviewees, whether of the left or right, is that economists are "useful" *because* they are pluralist. They see academic economics as intrinsically pluralist and are more accepting of the discipline's pluralism than politicians from other countries, who complain that economists should be more united. French politicians' acceptance of economics pluralism manifests in two ways. First, many who studied economics at university describe being exposed to many schools. There is some disagreement as to whether economics at French universities is more or less mathematical than at UK universities, with some interviewees having attended in both countries. However, there is a common tendency for former students of economics to say that there was an "eclectic" mix of "Keynesian", "liberal" and even "Marxist" teaching.

Second, economics in the present is also eclectic, albeit perhaps in a different way. The "old schools" continue. But they have been added to since the 2008 financial crisis, stemming from attempts to explain secular stagnation and environmentalist economics: a "structuring evolution of economic thought". I note at the start of the chapter that many politicians say economic ideas have become more eclectic again in the last ten or so years in the political domain, and there is widespread recognition of this trend by politicians. One LREM politician who invites economists to address his committee makes a virtue of having "a vision as large as possible". He claims that French economists are becoming better at leaving their universities to engage with politicians, as American and British economists such as Joseph Stiglitz, Paul Krugman and Robert Rubin do. He mentions the "sweet spot" where some young French economists, such as Stéfanie Stantcheva, have international careers and "do not hesitate to write about political economy". One LREM politician comments that, in the pandemic, the problem has been that "generations read the present based on what they thought before", but the pandemic has forced them to shake up their existing reading grids and "find the analyses that are quite free from the ideological framework that prevailed before". It is difficult for older economists to do this, and he therefore finds himself drawing on the younger ones. One example that he mentions, echoing a couple of the German interviewees, is behavioural economics, "led a little bit by the UK and the US". He thinks it may have value in incentivizing changes towards more environmentalist behaviours. In his own case, his liberal predispositions in economics have been challenged, because – as a politician in the governing party, responding to the crisis – he has to work out what is "efficient", from a social as well as an economic point of view.

French interviewees are not united on which economists they rely on. Some on the left hope there will still be economists who can keep the "grand theory" going, rather than new and innovative approaches such as behavioural economics. Some believe "European" economic thought needs to become more integrated, not maintained in national silos. Some are less pluralist than others. They may say they welcome the pluralism but actually consistently draw on one group of economists in practice. Nevertheless, as a group, French politicians are far more respectful of the plurality of economics than politicians in any of the other four countries.

However, their respect for the pluralism of economists makes it unlikely that they will find a unified body of opinion of experts they could agree to cede power to. Over and over again the French interviewees claim that economics is not a "hard" science. Like the majority of interviewees, they see politicians rather than economists as responsible: politicians seeking out a wide range of economist voices, but then having to decide. As one centre-right politician concludes:

Economists are useful because they give a point of view, a point of view like the trade unionists can give … their vision of things over the long term. But, for me, I'm always going to distinguish a point of view – advice, if I can call it that – from the decision. And the decision is political. It's elected officials who are elected for that reason: that they have to take the decisions … I've sometimes – often, even – decided not to follow [economists'] advice because the social, cultural and economic approaches, at the same time, appeared to me to yield different decisions.

They do not want to become experts themselves – another problem with the thesis that Macron was introducing "technocracy". As one LREM politician says:

So, I don't think that the parliamentarian's role, except if he has a very technical role in the Finance Commission or something of this type … is to be a technical expert in the economy. I think his role is to try and understand how he can fulfil his public policy objectives through the instruments given to him. I cannot say that it would be a bad thing to have economic training, but I don't think that it would be something that would fundamentally turn the tide.

Relationship between responsibility and responsiveness

As we have seen in Chapter 3, when we ask how politicians think voters see the economy, politicians answer fairly neutrally that they see it from the perspective of their own well-being. This perception of voters' narrow self-interest is also true in France. However, French politicians go on to speak more negatively about voters than those in the other four countries in these four respects. First, they are more likely than in the other countries to interpret voters' lack of wider economic interest and knowledge as a problem. For instance, a centre-right politician's first comment is that voters see the economy as "the most complete fog". They are less likely than British politicians in particular to praise voters' common sense or awareness of conditions on the ground. An LREM politician says that in France the state is now so integrated in society (he uses the example of a state-backed savings scheme) that voters need to be able to understand the state in order to understand the economy. This leads French voters to have a lower level of economic understanding, and hence standard of economic debate, than in other countries. He thinks that "British voters, Danish voters, countries with a more liberal tradition, have a rather good instinctive conception of the economy combined with a quite simple ideological prism, which separates the two, and puts on one side the liberal economy and on another side a protective role of the state, such as in Sweden or Denmark". The problem in France is the Colbertist tradition, "where the state is an economic actor", making the reading of the interaction between state and economy very complicated. These French politicians might be surprised at the extent to which British and Danish politicians in our study point to the same narrow self-interest of voters as French politicians, but not surprised that they talk more of voters having common-sense understandings of the economy.

Second, some, usually on the right, argue that excessive dependence on the state has built up a problem regarding voters' expectations. Sometimes they combine this tendency with what they describe as a French obsession with equality. A centre-right politician says voters both over- and underestimate what politicians can achieve economically. Voters find it "convenient" to unload demands for increased salaries and jobs onto politicians. "But, at the same time, the voter underestimates – distrusts, even, sometimes – the work of politics."

Third, many interviewees are worried that voters will turn to populists offering easy solutions. Yellow vest protests are sometimes offered as an example. One left politician says a party such as LREM talks about the economy instinctively and often, whereas with a party such as the Rassemblement National and the economy "there's not much doing". A centre-right politician talks about voter distrust, which has been increasing, leading to "political discourse not being credible anymore". One left-wing politician says that, because voters are anxious about the economy but also do not understand it, they reach a point at which they will not listen to politicians' talk but pay attention only to actions, results, which he describes as a hollow kind of pragmatism.

> And the danger from that is that there's a global condemnation of everyone [centrist], of all the left and the right who talk about the economy and make decisions, and thus that feeds the most total thinking, the most extreme, whether it's ultra-statist, on the extreme left ... or on the extreme right. And this is surely one of the main causes, this kind of failure of reflection, and of constructive debate around economic policy, which explains the rise in power of a number of authoritarian governments, or ... authoritarian parties.

Fourth, they are preoccupied with a feature of French politics they call "immobilisme" (resistance to change), which has made economic policy-making difficult, compounding voter distrust. Some believe voters feel that

France is in a permanent state of economic crisis. A centre-right politician says it is now between ten and 20 years since the start of the financial crisis, and in all that time "public opinion has been living with the idea that there is a crisis that we cannot get out of", although this is less true in Germany and northern Europe. This critique comes most often from the right and LREM. One centre-right politician says that, when his party was in government, "we tried to move things along. But we didn't succeed in moving them enough." He blames the "paralysing" historic administrative burdens and regulation. The "egalitarianism" of the voters reinforces administrative burdens because people insist on everyone being treated in the same way. It amounts to a "tyranny of the status quo". A second centre-right politician echoes this sentiment when he says the Germans have already made a lot of reforms, meaning they can more easily meet new challenges. He has the most evocative description of immobilisme. He accepts that some progress has been made in the last 20 years, but

> [i]t's clear that we are always circling around the same subjects. You take the issues of ten years ago, seen as a huge problem. You look back to see if it has been reduced, and it has not. That's pretty terrifying if you are a politician – right? It's always the same issues, it's the same questions, it's the same diagnoses, the same paths towards a solution, but it's not moving.

LREM politicians think they have started to tackle immobilisme; one says: "We showed it was possible to have an impact." Like many other politicians, he claims the distrust and disillusionment feed apathy as well as support for populists. However, he also cites the impact of "globalization and the victory of neoliberalism", giving voters the impression "there was not much to do". One of his LREM colleagues cautions against an approach that is too "economically liberal", in the sense of being focused on efficiency at the expense of social issues. As a consequence of phenomena such as Brexit, his younger generation of politicians "has become more and more conscious that certain economic choices can be economically efficient but can lead in the medium term to harmful political consequences". Prior decisions taken by Tony Blair's Labour government in the UK to accept EU migration were positive from an economic perspective, but then contributed to the Brexit decision, which is negative from an economic perspective. This perception distinguishes LREM from the more liberal approach of British Conservatives, who tend to claim that their sound management of economic policy will automatically lead to social benefits (even if some argue they violated that approach when they took the Brexit path).

The sense of voters being shut out from debate about economic policy-making during the neoliberal era is one aspect that left-wing politicians also look at when they are diagnosing voter distrust. A far-left politician says, "The economy is often presented as intangible data, as a dogma." Often in the neoliberal era voters were given the impression that economic policy was not up for discussion, because either there was only one path or it was too subject to globalizing forces. But the far left, when it was too "statist" and shut voters out of decision-making, was also at fault. The key now is for there to be a democratic debate including "democratization" of the economy in the form of greater worker control. The far-left politician says, "Economic policy *is* part of political debate, and we need economic policy choices to be decided by citizens. So we need to put economic policy at the heart of the political debate."

Many, from left and right, call for economic education. This does not have to be formal, at the school level; it could also be in the shape of politicians and others framing economic messages in less technical terms and giving voters the impression that there is a "democratic" debate to be had. An LREM politician hopes for economists who can help educate. A former teacher who is now a centre-right politician says more politicians like her are needed – "politicians who know have to speak to voters, taking them as intelligent people, capable of understanding, who can explain quite complicated things, but in a simple way".

Conclusion

French politicians' ideas about what makes responsible economic policies, in the long-term interest, were divergent in the past, in the days of "grand theories", and have become so again since the 2008 financial crisis. They contest those economic ideas hotly. There are no signs that Macron's presidency has succeeded, as one claimed, to make them all blend into a "casserole".

This divergence in ideas is one reason that, as they face even more complex economic pressures in the coming years, they are unlikely to agree to cede control over economic policy to outside experts. A second reason is that, although they are attentive to and respectful of economists, more so than in the other four countries apart from Denmark, the respect is of a certain kind. It is respect for a pluralist discipline, a soft science, comparable with philosophy or sociology in how divided it is. They do not object to that division, but it makes it unlikely that they will agree on which experts to trust who had anything like a unified consensus. They would prefer to get the advice and make their own minds up. They prefer to keep the economists as external advisers. Finally, they may be pessimistic about immobilisme, voter distrust and the populist threat, but not one offers up the technocratic solution – of ceding power to independent experts – as a solution to populism. Instead, however wearily, they argue that they will have to explain economic policies better. As I show in Chapter 9, the French politicians are among those most determined to become "educators".

7

Inattentive Anglosphere right

I mean, Trump really had no economic plan, except to do what was easy and popular, so: cut taxes, raise spending ... It will certainly continue to have an influence, but it is not well thought out; there's no intellectual base or reasoning for what he did. (Republican politician)

You want well-paid jobs, you want more people to be able to save in the future, buy nice homes, do things they take pleasure in. So, you're obviously working away to increase opportunity to try and get general overall economic growth. At the highest levels there should be a lot of agreement, and much of the strongly contested disagreement is about the means by which you pursue that.

(Conservative politician, former minister)

I have grouped American Republicans with British Conservatives because their way of thinking about the economy is similar, in the sense that they share a liberal economic heritage that is distinct from the more Christian tradition of the centre right in France, Germany and Denmark. Transatlantic links between economists and politicians are strong. Both Republicans and Conservative interviewees see the period of the Reagan and Thatcher governments as important watersheds in the movement from Keynesian to more market-conforming approaches. They confirm the judgement in much of the literature that market-conforming ideas have been more dominant in the "Anglosphere" than in continental Europe. First, I set out what the Republican interviewees say about their economic thinking and respect for economists, followed by the Conservatives. Surprisingly, given that their countries are home to neoclassical economics, they share a dismissive attitude to economists. But their reasons for being dismissive are different.

Republican context

Donald Trump was elected US president in 2016 despite many economists warning that he did not have a credible economic platform. He ended up violating sacrosanct economic principles of the Republican Party, such as free trade and balanced budgets, before his economic programme was derailed by the pandemic. I worked very hard to find Republican interviewees who wholeheartedly supported his economic policies, but most, even if they had never publicly opposed him, did not support his increased borrowing and/or trade policies. Whether publicly for or against Trump, they saw him as a big economic departure for their party and were waiting to see what would happen next. Would their party return to what one described as the optimism of Reaganite economics, or would it stay with what many called the populism or demagoguery of Trumpist economics?

Even without a pandemic, sitting American politicians are hard to reach, surrounded by gatekeepers who guard every minute of their schedules. The main period for interviews, all of which were conducted online, was between April and August 2021. Most of those who agreed to talk to us had recently (in either the 2018 or 2020 elections) retired, or had lost their seats and were waiting to get back into elected office. I selected congressmen and -women who had served on "economic" committees, such as House Ways and Means. I supplemented the accounts of seven former representatives with two members of the Trump presidency executive and an adviser to a senior "economic" representative. The politicians are described according to whether they are in the "centrist" or "right" half of the Republican Party, according to websites, such as GovTrack, that track how politicians vote, combined with their self-assessments. I also give details of where their districts are, such as "Midwest", to help the reader track their accounts.

According to Fourcade (2009), economists are more powerful in the United States than in any other country. They are "merchant professionals" (Fourcade 2009: ch. 2), who have secured positions in universities and the business world that have earned them money and status. She describes the awesome power of American economists worldwide. Economics is seen as worth studying at university level; in 2019 a total of 48,297 degrees in economics were awarded to citizens and permanent residents of the United States.[1] Liberal arts students often study at least a couple of compulsory economics modules. Fourcade's explanation for US economists' domestic power is that the centrality of the market leads to a certain kind of respect for individuals who have skills to

---

1. See https://datausa.io/profile/cip/economics.

analyse it. Therefore, I expected the American Republicans to respect the authority of economists. However, partisanship has accelerated in recent years, and some on the American right increasingly see economists as left-leaning, unless they come from business schools or key universities where pro-market ideas are still seen as dominant. The Council of Economic Advisers, according to Campbell and Pedersen, flip-flopped in its advice during the decades between the 1980s and 2007, depending on whether a Republican or Democrat administration was in power, reflecting what they describe as a "highly partisan war" of economic ideas (2014: 300). Even though they flip-flopped, they were consistently more "neoliberal" than their counterpart councils in Germany, Denmark and France.

In this chapter I argue that US right-wingers may usually be associated with "free markets" and a certain kind of attachment to efficiency that was exemplified by some economists from the neoliberal era, but their economic goals are more normative than that characterization suggests. In addition, they are less attentive to economists than any of the other groupings. They do not seem likely to espouse arguments for economic technocracy. But they are highly focused on their responsiveness to voters, including on communicating economic messages to them.

Republicans' communication with voters

Whatever the case in the broader population, few members of the House of Representatives or the Senate have economics degrees; most, as in other parliaments, still have a law background (Bonica 2017; Kramer 2017). A few of our interviewees have business qualifications but they say that these did not have a strong economics component. One, the first Midwesterner Republican, with a science background, says he is unusual: "Most of these folks are attorneys. They come from a background that doesn't really have an economic perspective or real-world experience, or a lot haven't even worked in in business." He says his fellow representatives' lack of economic knowledge makes economic policy-making "challenging", and he works hard to produce briefings for them so that they can become better informed. However, he is the only Republican politician to diagnose representatives as lacking economic knowledge and see it as a problem.

Our Republicans interviewees may have similar goals to those of neoclassical market-conforming economists, and beliefs in the value of free markets, but they think about them in different ways. We have seen in Chapter 4 that the left tends to have normative goals, and that also seems a dominant feature for politicians in Denmark and for German right-wingers. But it is also true for US Republicans. They often say that there is a value in working hard and independently of the state, which made them predisposed towards entrepreneurialism or free markets, and that this is in itself a "value" that goes beyond their efficiency.

When I ask Republican politicians "When did you first become aware of the economy?", they mostly respond with teenage memories of receiving their first pay cheque. This contrasts with other politicians in the study, who respond with memories of their families' economic circumstances, not their own earning potential. What seems to be key in the case of American Republicans is that, in a country where there is not much of a safety net, what they themselves can earn will be crucial. A Southwesterner's story about his first pay cheque is an emotional one with a moral undercurrent about the value of work. He says his family were poor rural workers who "never had enough". At the age of nine he got a job before and after school with a farmer.

> The farmer would pick me up at 4:30 in the morning, we'd go out and we'd work until 7:00. He'd take me home, I'd get on the bus, go to school, then come back, and he'd pick me up in the afternoon. I can remember, two weeks after I started, he pulls up, he reaches over and pulls this dusty old book out. I didn't know. My folks had a [small] chequebook, little bitty cheques. This one was kind of a three-ring binder, and I've never seen anything like that. I thought he must have owned the bank! And when he got out and he wrote that cheque out and filled that thing out and put my name in there, asked me how to spell my name, it was one of the most significant moments of my life. I realized that, if you work, then there are people who will compensate you for that work.

The realization that people would reward him for working gave him the first sense of his potential to attain both freedom and security. He describes his personal goal as having been "prosperity", which is "far more than money in the bank": "It's a sense of satisfaction, a sense of belief that it's going to be okay, that I can start a career ... I can find fulfilment through advancement, I can know that I can go buy a house and pay for it over time."

Republicans talk about the goal of the pursuit of prosperity as being about character and what gives life meaning. They use the language of risk, reward and – relatedly – incentive a lot, but in these moralistic terms. Rewards when you have earned them by your own efforts are greater; as a first Florida representative says, you will "appreciate" them. A third Midwesterner says that, if you want to get the rewards from the risks you take, you also "have to accept the downside", that sometimes you will not be rewarded and that it should not be the role of government to bail you out. He is also a strong Christian, and believes that "when an individual works hard to do better for themselves they're [also] doing better for their community", because they are helping to generate prosperity and jobs in it.

At first glance, the third Midwesterner seems to be describing his free-market beliefs in ways that would echo a supply-side economist. He looks out over manufacturing plants that have closed down in his small town and semi-rural district. He is enough of a believer that markets should be free from government interference to have accepted their closure and to have consistently opposed state intervention to save businesses, including voting against some of the bailouts following the 2008 crisis. However, he extends his analysis in more sociological and moralistic directions than economists. For instance, he believes city dwelling, where "too many people are too crowded together", is what leads people to "look for government to help". But "my folks", his small-town constituents, do not look for government to help.

> I just think that they live pretty simply ... They don't ask for very much, you know, they don't want government around. So, it's really kind of a throwback to the kind of the development of our country where you kept moving west to kind of get away, and you saved your ground and you held your ground and you'll maybe pass it on to the next generation. I think there's still a little bit of that left.

He concludes, "We're a country that still believes in the individual and the power of the individual and self-determination, and all those corny words."

Similarly, although several talk explicitly about the need to keep the American dream alive, that risk, talent and effort will be rewarded, they are less worried that its decline will damage economic efficiency than that it will erode broader norms that keep societies harmonious. The first Midwesterner is concerned that low growth is undermining the American dream. He says that low growth has caused an increase in "class envy" for the first time in the history of the United States, manifest in what he sees as unfair attacks on billionaires and "the 1 per cent". In the past, when people witnessed success, "the reason people weren't jealous was they thought: 'That could be me; that could be my grandchildren; that could be my children.' Some of that is waning now, obviously, and this shine is off of that penny somewhat, which is unfortunate."

Trump's Tax Cuts and Jobs Act

Although Republicans think that attachment to free markets is a dominant idea in their country, they believe they need to be ever vigilant in persuading voters. They refer often to some of their narratives being hard for voters to understand. The first example of a message that Republican interviewees consistently preach is the need for fiscal conservatism. They welcome the tax cuts in President Trump's Tax Cuts and Jobs Act and believe they stimulated growth. However, a majority argue that the tax cuts should have been designed to have a less dramatic impact on revenues in the short term. They believe the Laffer curve effect, of rising receipts from growth induced by tax cuts, was proved to be right in the Reagan era and would have followed the Trump cuts, even if it had taken a little time.[2] They would have preferred the Trump tax cuts to have been accompanied by cuts – or, at least, not rises – in spending. Instead, Trump told voters they could have both: tax cuts and increased spending, paid for out of increased borrowing.

Self-styled fiscal conservative Republican interviewees believe the increased debt is irresponsible and will lead to economic damage, such as inflation. But Trump's abandonment of fiscal conservatism will also mean that Republicans find it harder to preach tough messages about spending in future. A centrist Republican, the second to have represented Florida, echoes many of the Republican interviewees in describing Trump as "populist", and says that this populist message on borrowing will be part of his "legacy". He believes that, "long term, economic ideas and policies have to have a solid base where things can be explained, and they make sense". Voters can understand a (Republican) case that says "We want to keep taxes low and limit the role of government so that private companies and entrepreneurs can flourish and provide new jobs and opportunities for people". Equally, they can understand a case, more likely to be made by Democrats, that taxes need to be raised on the wealthy. But Trump's message – "We just need to cut taxes as low as possible and increase spending and we'll just keep borrowing money" – undermines the sense of the original Republican message, and what the centrist Republican sees as "economic reality". He says Trump has "debased the currency of economic ideas". He has in his mind that the Trump borrowing message is comparable to the Democrat-led message that everyone could own their own homes, which he thinks fuelled the 2008 financial crisis. His concern, echoed by many others, is therefore that the "incoherence", "lack of rigour" or "lack of ideological foundation" of Trump's economic ideas in themselves undermine the messages that are needed to keep

---

2. Arthur Laffer (of curve fame) is in fact the economist mentioned most often by Republicans.

voters attached to the free market. This amounts to "populism", which is also "unsustainable" and will eventually lead "to some sort of crisis".

Trump's trade policies

Trump's assault on free trade is the second case study to illustrate interviewees' concern about how he undermined necessary economic messages. Most interviewees link free markets and free trade inextricably. A mid-Atlantic Republican says, "I certainly support *free markets; that would include opening markets for trade.*" He goes as far as to say that "protectionism is a form of crony capitalism", because it "protects the few at the expense of the many". When I ask the first Midwesterner about his economic values, he says he believes in free trade as a "bedrock principle of Republican economics". As a Republican adviser says, Republicans were known as more attached to free trade than Democrats, and free-trade beliefs "used to be sacrosanct in the party". The interviewees are more damning of Trump in the sections of their interviews when they talk about his trade policies than about his increased borrowing. It is in the context of talking about his opposition to Trump's protectionism that the third Midwesterner makes his strongest criticism of Trump: "Trump is really a populist; he wasn't really a Republican. I had a reporter tell me 'It was like a hostile takeover of the party'. I said: 'Yeah!'"

Concern about China and how free trade was closing down US manufacturing had been making voters increasingly disposed to protectionism, and many interviewees say Trump was over-responsive to them and "demagogued" the issue. The Republican adviser says that it has always been "tough" to get across the pro-trade message to voters who think free trade is responsible for job losses, but Trump made their job harder. The third Midwesterner echoes this line of thought:

> [Free trade] is a tough argument. I mean, from my house, I can look and see a steel mill … But my free-trade position is that lower costs of goods and services benefit everybody, and then you manufacture in the area of the world that's the most efficient. We can make brooms out of corn – right? Which we used to do, I think; I had plants all over this district. We were like the popcorn and the broom factory capital of the world … But it's cheaper to make raw brooms in Mexico, so that's where it went. But now, for those people in that community who are no longer making brooms, it's tough to go in there and tell them this free-market argument. But I just believe it works, and, I mean, it really lifts everybody up.

Do Republican interviewees show that they think like economists? First, the firmness of their belief in the law of comparative advantage, as outlined by the third Midwesterner, suggests that they do. However, some of their interpretive gloss on that law is that it has been particularly relevant to the United States as a large country. They interpret the historical evidence about US success in the global economy as evidence that that law works. Second, their criticisms of Trump's populist "economic incoherence" suggest that they think like economists more than he does. But they link the economic concepts with broader societal issues and express their thoughts in normative ways, using "corny" words. As I show in the next section, they do not attribute their beliefs to economists or show them much respect.

Republicans not respecting economists' authority: partisanship

Although Fourcade (2009) believes that Americans' respect for markets leads them to respect economists, she does also note that there is an interesting tension between what would usually be considered the objective and (in her terms) "professional" aspect of university-based economists and how easily economists move into the business or political world, helping "different groups with public claims fight one another" (Fourcade 2009: 9). I argue that she does not focus enough on how, in their interactions with the world of politics, economists might become infected with the high levels of partisanship that has been developing in US politics (McCarty 2019; Mason 2018). In these interviews conducted in 2021, 12 years after Fourcade wrote, when I ask "How useful do you find economists?" the only positive responses from Republicans are to "*conservative* economists" or even "*Republican* economists". As the third Midwesterner says, "And you've got *conservative ones* and *liberal ones*. You've got, you know, the Keynesians, and you've got the supply-side folks, and then you have the other folks."

American Republicans mention economists' names positively far less often than any other group of politicians in this study. Many of the British references are to economists they paid attention to only in their youth, such as US economist Milton Friedman. But American Republicans do not even credit Friedman with the neoliberal economic turn they welcomed in the 1970s and 1980s. Only one Republican politician mentions Friedman by name, compared with six British right-wingers. They are far more likely to say that President Reagan was the key influence on their early economic ideas. One reason for the lower Republican mention of named economists may be their current distrust of a discipline that at least two say is now "left-leaning".

At the same time, they show a lack of respect for the "conservative economists" they find useful because they treat them in a transactional way. Rather than listening to their advice, they tend to use them, such as on committees, to provide data to support pre-decided solutions or to counter their opponents' arguments. The third Midwesterner Republican again says, "So, I think whatever position you want to promote, you can get an economist to testify on that. Then the way it works in the House of Representatives, I'm sure on the Senate side too."

Therefore, because US politicians pay such low levels of attention to academic economists who might still maintain political neutrality, when asked for their views on "economists" the only ones that come to mind are those who are employed by their party machines, or gain work because they are linked with their party in some way. Technocrats might say this is precisely why a bigger role for the "objective" economists is needed: the current transactional approach to "using" experts is a corrupted one. However, what these interviews suggest is that politicians do not appear to have the residual respect for the profession that would be necessary to make that leap.

British Conservatives

I started interviewing Conservatives early in lockdown, in March 2020, when people were in their most panicked state. Some were still in their House of Commons offices, but the corridors were far quieter than they were used to. The division about whether lockdown should be lifted was intense; Rishi Sunak launched the "Eat out to help out" scheme in the summer, but it was clear by early autumn that normality would not return until enough people had been vaccinated. One interviewee in July told me to get back to my London office to boost economic activity, saying that "we need you there".

The Conservative government led by Boris Johnson had been re-elected in 2019 with a large majority, having won over former Labour voters in so-called "red wall" seats in the North. Johnson promised to "get Brexit done" and "level up" and purged the party of pro-Remain MPs, who were often also "economic liberals". Commentators speculated as to the way the purged party would go. In Andrew Gamble's (2017) words, would it follow the "global Britain" economic liberal path, or a "protectionist Britain" path that would somehow find money for social spending on levelling up? The Conservative interviewees are a mix; some describe themselves as Remainer economic liberals, others Brexiteers, and some fully embrace the levelling-up agenda. I found less difference between Leave and Remain supporters within this group than I had anticipated.

Despite the high salience of Brexit in the period of our interviews, the economic ideas that the politicians gravitated towards were about the relationship between market and state, rather than the openness of the economy.[3] This group of eight politicians includes six who have served as ministers. To avoid constant repetition of the term "former minister", I have used other describing factors to help the reader track their comments, relating mostly to the geographical area they served, such as "southern", or "Home Counties".

One dominant theme in the literature about Conservatives is their pragmatism. In his recent book, Edmund Fawcett (2020) argues that Conservatives adapt to national conditions rather than following universal principles. Their approach has always been "pragmatic", which he defines as following "context-free maxims of wise government" (Fawcett 2020: 406), seeking solutions according to whether they work to achieve broad goals rather than sticking to one ideological position. He cites the classic pragmatism of Conservative thinker Anthony Quinton, who defined the task of government as "driving a car along a narrow, winding road" (Fawcett 2020: 406).

A second dominant theme, in the literature on economists, suggests that UK politicians will have a high degree of respect for economists' professional authority. British economists have more of an "amateur" history than their American counterparts (Fourcade 2009: ch. 3). John Maynard Keynes epitomizes what came out of this tradition, including the greater interest in questions of distributive justice than their US counterparts. Margaret Thatcher spearheaded, with Ronald Reagan, the adoption of more supply-side economics, later branded "neoliberal" and mostly coming from the University of Chicago. Since that time Conservative governments have usually adopted the approach that "there is no alternative" to market forces, including in the austerity period of George Osborne's chancellorship (2010 to 2016), which suggests that they may proclaim that they follow economists' lead. On the other hand, Thatcher was often seen as anti-intellectual, and her original dalliance with economists might have been self-serving, so as to engineer a shift in a right-wing direction and differentiate Conservatives from Keynesian Labour (Hall 1993). Therefore, key questions regarding British Conservatives are whether and how they are "pragmatic" in their economic thinking, how they rate the professional authority of economists and which ones they focus on.

---

3. I do not include the former UKIP politicians within this chapter. They have a quite distinctive approach to economic ideas in the sense that they alone deviate from the high priority our interviewees tend to give to economic questions. For the UKIP politicians, the question of exit from the European Union is of overriding importance. They talk about economic ideas in a more instrumental way, with the end goal of achieving a successful Brexit. Moreover, their Euroscepticism is not fundamentally an economic idea in itself.

Conservatives' lack of normativity

In answer to the question about whether she has economic "values", a former Conservative minister is uneasily aware of the tension between descriptive ideas about the economy, on the one hand, and values, on the other. She says she can separate her ideas from her political "values" "intellectually", the way economists might. However, "*as a politician* that becomes more difficult", and "they become very integrated". She is referring here to how political pressures to frame goals ideologically and also engage constantly in delineating them from political opponents make it harder to pursue what will work if it conflicts with values or broader political considerations. However, even this description of a struggle is unusual among Conservative interviewees, because most claim to have economic goals that are far less normative than any other grouping of politicians in this book.

The Conservatives describe their economic goals as a "strong economy", or "prosperity" or "growth". They are strongly committed to them, many implying that it was their economic goals, rather than, for instance, social ones, that drove them into politics. Conservatives' earliest economic memories are different from Republicans. They rarely mention their first pay cheques, although a couple mention their family's economic circumstances. More usually they say they became conscious of the UK's economic decline and wanted to help reverse it. The first Home Counties politician, a former minister, says, "So, yes, from a pretty early stage … my interest in politics tended to be focused on … 'How do you have a strong economy?'" Many who became involved in the late 1970s mention their distress at how weak the British economy was. A southern politician, a former minister, was marked by how "far down the league table" the UK was at that stage. He decided he had to become a foot soldier in a long-term project to make Britain economically "well performing".

The Conservatives all share a commitment to the free market as the means to achieve their goal of prosperity. Instead of describing their views as linked with an intellectual economic tradition, such as "economic liberalism", they prefer to call themselves "free marketeer[s]". For example, a Conservative backbencher notes, "I think I'm a pretty strong free-market person." Conservatives see "the free market" as neoclassical economists might: as the most efficient way to ensure prosperity. A southwest politician, a former minister, says, "My fundamental belief in the marketplace – that, when properly regulated and properly used by the state, it is an engine of prosperity – remains undiminished." There is less emphasis than their Republican counterparts on "risk and reward", more on using phrases such as "the market is efficient in allocating resources". The term "free market" is not accompanied by the broader moral messages of the Republicans. A former minister and Brexiteer exemplifies the reluctance to talk about values in relation to the economy. He laughs somewhat uncomfortably and says, "I have values, yes; not economic values particularly, but values, yes." His hesitation is attributable to his complete commitment to the good of material growth. When probed about his commitment to the goal of prosperity, he becomes irritated:

> I want the consumer to be better off, not worse off. And for every middle-class consumer who may feel they've got enough goods and services I can take you to someone who isn't in that lucky position, who is not on your income or mine, and would like to have more scope to buy nice things or go somewhere interesting or whatever is on their to do list.

He believes all politicians should have the goal of "working ... to try and get general overall economic growth".

These Conservative politicians are the only ones in the study to use phrases such as "run" or "manage" the economy. Governments must avoid making "a mess" of running the economy. They also portray the economy as something further beyond their control than the other groups, with reference to "business cycles" or "markets" having more effect than their policies. Therefore, it would be tempting to argue that Conservatives think more like economists than many other groups of politicians. But it is more accurate to argue that they are pragmatic in their approach to "running" the economy. Conservatives oppose what they call "ideology". Many economists would argue that an anti-ideological stance is positive if it means politicians are shunning political ideology, but the politicians use the term to demonstrate more that they shun all economic theory. For instance, most of the interviewees say they believed national debt was too high by the time they took over government from Labour in 2010, and it needed to come down to avoid the UK being demoted in credit ratings. They supported chancellor of the Exchequer Osborne's austerity programme even though it caused welfare benefit and other cuts. However, they think it went too far and is an example of the danger of over-attachment to an ideology of fiscal consolidation and commitment to a small state. The first Home Counties politician and former minister believes this was a mistake; the Treasury team won "a big political and economic argument about the need to get borrowing down a bit faster than our opponents were going to do". However, winning this argument "essentially consumed the whole of, first, the Conservative Party and, then, the coalition government's political rhetoric". As a result, it "crowded out" all other arguments.

More recently, after the interviews, the government announced an even more dramatic change in economic policy direction, towards what Johnson called a "high-wage" economy (October 2021 party conference). This chimes with what some interviewees report as a modification of their economic goals, which also sets this group apart from the others in this study, who do not tend to report change at the "goal" level. A third of Conservative interviewees state explicitly that they have modified their economic goals in the last decade. Some report increasing enthusiasm for state intervention over the years, compared with views they held in the 1970s and 1980s. A southern politician and former minister says, "Gradually you discover that government also has got a useful role and there are legitimate roles of government." The first Home Counties politician and former minister echoes this view:

> One thing where perhaps my views have perhaps moved a little bit over the years is it doesn't necessarily follow that market economics requires a very small state … You can still have quite pro-market policies with a relatively large state … [T]here is an important role for the state in ensuring that markets work and, indeed, for taking into account those areas where there is a market failure.

Some have also modified the goal of "prosperity" that they had in the 1970s to take into account the need for a modest level of equity in its distribution. They usually attribute the modification to the changing economic circumstances of globalization exaggerating the gap between economic winners and losers and the need to be adaptable in light of secular stagnation after 2008. The southern politician and former minister says that, in the 1980s, economic growth could be the singular goal because "the surge" in incomes was felt by all, meaning the rise in inequality did not matter. In the more stagnant circumstances since 2008, "many of the gains are captured by the very rich" and it is "tough … for the less affluent". Increased inequality has become more of a problem, eroding social trust. A couple mention the need for stability. The "massively deflationary" circumstances since 2008 have convinced the southwest politician and former minister that "monetizing a huge part of the debt and injecting vast amounts of electronic money into the economy is a very good idea". In his youth he would have thought such an idea was heretical. He claims that "it's not really that my view about what might work under different circumstances has changed, but just the circumstances have changed". This third of interviewees claiming a change in economic goals is in contrast to the Republicans, none of whom say they have modified their goals.

Finally, unlike the Republicans, British Conservatives do not talk much about their commitment to free trade and the need to shore up public support for it. Instead, the core message is always common-sense materialist pursuit of prosperity and the Conservatives' greater skill in delivering it.

Conservative respect for professional authority

Conservative interviewees' attitudes to economists and their professional authority is complicated. First, they mention more economists than Republicans do. This may be related to the fact that a larger proportion of them compared with Republicans studied degrees with political economy in them. But, even though Conservatives mention economists more than Republicans, they still mention them less frequently than other groups in this study, such as the German right. And the ones they mention by name positively tend to be limited to Milton Friedman and "monetarists" and to be portrayed as a youthful stage they went through that they then grew out of. They also often mention the vague commitment to "free-market economists" without specifying names. The southern politician explains that there are two elements to Friedman's monetarism: a school of thought about controlling inflation, which they soon discarded; and a strengthened predisposition towards free markets, which endured.

A couple of the Conservatives show respect for economists as "objective", in contrast to Republicans. The southwest politician says that, "if by 'economic thinking' you mean theorizing about particular causes and effects", then he does not think his "particular political views, in the sense of my views about what it's desirable to try to achieve in our society, imply any particular set of economic theories", because economists in the neoclassical canon at any rate are in his view objective, concerned only to achieve efficiency. He says he would consult economic theories, but in the spirit of empirical open-mindedness: "I mean, I, if something isn't working, try something else. And, if the something else doesn't work, try something again else, and it actually does work [so] keep trying it [laughs]." If he had announced this stance in public he would have lost voter confidence, but in private, given that economists often cannot agree about what effects different policies will have, he believes that pragmatism is "the rational stance".

However, most Conservatives do not bother to pay attention to economists, either because they see them as divided or too "theoretical". They search for the policies that will work to achieve the general goal of prosperity wherever they can find it. They favour "applied" studies, including watching where their opponents' policies in government, such as the minimum wage or raising tax thresholds, have "worked". Indeed, they are anti-theoretical. A second Home Counties politician, also a former minister, says he is "sceptical of theory on its own" and values "applied policies and ideas": "I valued X years in the private sector before going into politics, because it meant I understood the dynamics of the marketplace. And therefore, when I came to apply theoretical policies ... it was saying, 'Will this actually work in the real world?' And that, I think, is a really important test."

This preference for the practical is not unique to the right in Britain; a former Labour minister says that "one of the advantages over theoretical economists that finance ministers have is that you're following a dose of common sense", for example. But the Conservatives seem more overtly distrustful of theoretical approaches, whereas their Labour Party counterparts are more likely to recognize the need for other inputs in addition.

Conclusion

Republicans are strongly committed to "free-market" ideas and achieving prosperity, but they do not express the high levels of respect for the economics profession and its relevance compared with other right-wing parties, such as the German CDU/CSU. They do not follow a particular school of (neoclassical) economics in the way that the German CDU/CSU follows the ordoliberals, or the centre left follows Keynesianism. Most have not read "big name" economists, such as Milton Friedman, whereas their British counterparts are more likely, in their study of history or politics, to have studied what could be described as "political economy" in the form of Keynes's or Friedman's impact. Republicans' transactional use of economists, such as their partisan advisers, is striking. Republicans do not seem to respect the authority of "independent" economists in the way technocrats would hope for.

At the same time, economic ideas in the United States are diverging and deeply contested. Although many on the left in Europe would consider American Democrats to be only mildly left in their economic ideas, as we have seen in Chapter 4, progressive Democrats are arguing strongly for redistribution, and Republican interviewees refer to this as a dangerous leftward shift in economic ideas within the United States. Moreover, Republicans are themselves increasingly divided on economic issues such as free trade, as a result of the protectionist moves by Trump. This contestation makes it unlikely that politicians in the United States will choose to go down a technocratic route, because they would not be able agree on which economists to cede power to.

Are US Republicans "over-responsive" to voters, so that technocrats might argue that a degree of cession of control to experts would be desirable, on the grounds that it would lead to more responsible government? On the subject of over-responsiveness, some interviewees argue that Trump represents a populist threat, simplifying and degrading economic debate. But these Republicans as a whole take their responsive duties as economic communicators more seriously than he does. They give the impression of always having had to work harder, certainly than the British right, on economic messaging. Superficially, the dominant voter predisposition is an attachment to free markets and rugged individualism that suits them well. But, on closer inspection, Republican politicians have not taken attachment to the American dream or free trade for granted. And in recent years, with the assault on some of their economic beliefs in part from their own president, they have had to draw on strategies to communicate and engage with voters even more vigorously. Although these interviewees, having answered our invitation to take part in academic research about economic ideas, are likely to be more responsible communicators than some of their colleagues, it is striking that they take engagement with voters on economic issues to be important to democracy. They recognize that voter disengagement, or leaving the stage to simpler non-economic messages, would be damaging.

I found that, of all the groups in the study, it is the British Conservatives who had the least normative economic goals, talking more about "managing" the economy. The way they talk about free markets, as the efficient way to achieve prosperity, is less normative in tone compared with American Republicans. In addition, a greater number than on the US side say they have modified their goals away from a pure free-market position in recent years. They show more respect for the professional authority of (neoclassical) economists than American Republicans, in the sense that they have read more of them and acknowledge them as objective, not divided into partisan camps. But the respect is superficial, because they are explicitly "anti-theoretical" in their assessment of how useful economists are. They do not rate the formalization and abstraction of economists highly, preferring what has been tested in real-world conditions, whichever body of economic thought it comes from. British Conservatives pay little attention to the principles or beliefs about causation that guide those schools and are open-minded in seeking out any policy that will "work". British Conservatives are some of the least attentive to and respectful of economists, and the most practically orientated of politicians, unlikely to cede power to economic experts. At the same time, they are some of the most respectful towards voters, rarely criticizing their lack of knowledge in judgemental terms. Nevertheless, the British approach is not to engage in depth with voters but to trust to a reputation for economic competence.

8

Politicians and climate change economists

But new changes have come forward on the agenda of everyone; "Remember the climate", for instance, changing totally what's really good economic policy.   (Danish Social Democrat politician)

A number of politicians advocate "degrowth". I don't believe that it is possible for a country like France, who's seen mass unemployment. I think we have an obligation today to continue to create jobs … perhaps not in the same way, and certainly not to have growth that is so demanding in the consumption of resources, but I think we must continue to produce, to be a country that builds, that creates businesses. So, on these issues, my position is very classically a position, I would say, more of the liberal right, which believes in business. There's the path: entrepreneurial freedom, freedom of initiative, believing in innovation and in research progress. Things which have sometimes been abandoned, including by the left.

(French centre-right politician)

Economist Kate Raworth (2017) says that "you can't walk away from economics because it frames the world we inhabit", but decided we need to "flip it on its head": "What if we started economics with humanity's goals for the 21st century, and then asked what economic mindset would give us even half a chance of achieving them?" She develops the doughnut concept of boundaries, in which the hole in the middle is where people's needs are not met and the boundary beyond the edge of the doughnut is where we risk putting too much pressure on the world's resources. Drawing on numerous strands of economics, such as "complexity, ecological, feminist, behavioural and institutional economics", her aim is to find how to meet humanity's needs. But she says it will require a fundamental transformation of the "mainstream economic mindset", from universities to parliaments.

So far, this book has related how politicians describe their current economic mindsets. Most recount a chronological path, starting in their late teens or early twenties, of becoming interested in politics, becoming aware of their own values and predispositions and how this process affected their thinking about the economy. It may be that future books on politicians who grew up in conditions of climate crisis will find that it shaped their economic thinking from the outset more profoundly, but I believe the approach taken in this book, of asking politicians about their "economic ideas" without framing the whole interview as being about the economics of the environment, gives us an accurate sense of how much today's politicians have changed their mindset. It leads us to the conclusion, set out in this chapter, that, whatever might happen in the future to politicians' beliefs about the need to mitigate climate change, their current mindset as to how to achieve whatever it is they want to achieve in this respect through economic means is mostly still tacked onto how they have always thought about the economy.

The interviewees diverge in how much they have even thought about the environment, how far it is to the forefront of their minds. Some on the right still see the environment as tangential to the economy, an issue that can be solved through private-sector-driven technology or innovation that does not need much state intervention or adaptation of broader policies. Others on the right have "long-term" thinking at the core of their economic thinking already, and claim to have incorporated the concept of environmental sustainability into it. Of those who think economic policy does need to be modified, they diverge on the extent.

Only a small group respond fully to Kate Raworth's call to fundamentally change their mindsets. They argue that the environment should replace notions of the economy. Instead of thinking about how to produce and distribute natural resources in a "sustainable" way, they say we should be thinking about what the purpose of production and distribution is in a radical "*socio*-ecological restructuring". As you would expect, politicians in each of the three groups who follow economists' writings on the subject cite different economists as influencing their views.

However, in comparison to their more general economic ideas, although the *range* of politicians' ideas on the economics of the environment is as wide as we have seen in the general economic ideas throughout this book, more of the politicians cluster in the middle category. And, of course, some argue that the climate crisis itself could drive a shift towards enhanced support for state intervention. Therefore, I consider whether there might be more of a potential for a settled consensus on the economics of the environment than for broader economic ideas.

Contested and divergent ideas about the economics of the environment

Because I did not ask direct questions about the environment, the number of times interviewees raise the environment themselves gives strong insights into how far they think it is relevant to the economy. Having the reputation for being one of the countries most committed to environmentalism, I expected the Danes to bring the environment into the interviews the highest number of times out of all five countries. In the event, they nearly had the top spot, but were narrowly beaten by the Germans. However, this partly reflects how unproblematic Danish interviewees find their commitment to environmentalism and how far there is a relatively settled consensus view on its importance in Denmark. The German interviewees find that being at an earlier stage of making the transition from their more industrialized economy to a greener one is much more difficult, and therefore more to the forefront of their minds.

I should note that the pattern of questioning changed as the interviews progressed. I continued the practice of not asking directly about the environment through the first three sets of interviews, with the British, then the Germans, then the Danes. But by the time I got to the French and Americans I had developed a practice whereby, if they did not raise it, I would ask about it myself towards the end of the interview. Overall, the French raise it proactively, and often early in the interviews. US politicians raise it proactively far less frequently, so many of the responses from them that I set out here were in response to a direct question.

Across the five countries, interviewees fall into three categories in terms of how far environmental concerns are affecting their economic ideas. The first group sees the threat from climate change as only marginally affecting their economic ideas, either because they think the threat is not severe or because they think they can deal with it within their existing market-based economic paradigms. The second group have modified their responses to a greater extent. But this is a very large group that spans different approaches. For the third group, environmentalism should become the *basis* for economic thinking. Right-wing politicians who believe in free markets would find it impossible to subscribe to this view, because it re-visions a prosperous economy as one that fits within planetary environmental limits *and* fulfils "social needs", including social equity, and "socio-ecological" restructuring.

Marginally affected by environmental concerns

The first group either never raise the issue of the environment, indicating that they do not believe it is of importance in an interview about the economy, or, if they do mention climate change, imply they do not think it can be prevented, so the only relevant economic policy might be to do things such as insuring for flood risk. Some see climate change in the way some economic models have treated pollution: as a market externality that requires a response. However, they stress that the response should be as market-based as possible.

In the early interviews with the British and German politicians, when I do not prompt them with a question about the impact of the environment on the economy I get a direct comparison between the two right-wing parties. Several British Conservatives do not raise it any point, compared with nearly all CDU/CSU politicians, so I assume the Conservatives fall into this category. Most American Republicans, who I prompt with a direct question about how far the environment affects their economic thinking, fall into this category of having incorporated environmental considerations into their economic thinking only at the margins, or advocating policies that require minimal adaptation.

None of the interviewees in this group admit to being outright climate change deniers. However, a British Conservative criticizes climate change activism as cult-like and emotional: "And, if you ask people, do they know [the science], they just take it as tenet of faith. Faith has brought them to it. Faith in the nation state has gone, faith in God has gone, but, by goodness, we have faith in scientists who tell us that the environment is going to hell in a handcart." And some start their sentence with "I'm not a climate denier, but …", and go on to say that climate change is not as fast-paced as some scientists claim, or make a distinction that they are more concerned about threats to the environment in the shape of reduced biodiversity and the need for recycling than climate change.

I follow the distinction that scholars such as Dan Fiorino (2018) make between adapting to the effects of climate change and mitigating it, trying to prevent it happening. When it comes to what economic policy should be introduced, there is some support in this group for adapting to the effects of climate change, such as changing insurance policy and building regulations. Many stress that the private sector has to lead here. But, on mitigating climate change, they are more circumspect. A Republican adviser says she will follow an "innovation and markets perspective". A French centre-right politician, echoed by a British Conservative, contrasts a desirable "liberal" market-driven vision with one that is punitive and constraining. One common theme in this group is that the economy should not "suffer" from environmental measures.

As one Republican expounds, "From an economic perspective, when those types of policy are looked at, it's important to look at them in the context of economic growth and not hurting your economy." Relatedly, they oppose action to mitigate climate change by developed nations such as theirs when China and India are not taking action on a comparable scale, because they may secure an economic advantage with cheaper and dirtier production processes. One Republican says he opposes redistribution generally, and developed nations should not "redistribute" to poorer nations in this way. And another calls developed nations taking the lead on climate change as a transfer of wealth and "posturing" rather than "serious policy-making".

Most Republicans have been suspicious of using tax, such as the carbon tax, to mitigate climate change. A Midwestern Republican says he is beginning to consider it and cites this fact as evidence for how rapidly opinion is shifting. It is interesting that he thinks voters are paying increasing attention to the environment. Nevertheless, to give an indication of how weak this kind of commitment still is within the party, he is the only Republican interviewee who wholeheartedly supports policies such as a carbon tax and subsidizing renewables that "promote both economic and environmental goals". Climate change consumes a lot of his time "and political capital", making him an "outlier" in his party.

It is noticeable that only right-wing politicians fall into this "marginally affected by environmental concerns" category. British Conservatives demonstrate inattention to the issue, by not proactively raising it, so perhaps if I had pressed them as I did the Republicans they might have advocated for support for economic policies to mitigate climate change. But American Republicans, when prompted, are nearly all sceptical or minimalist. By contrast, only a couple of the French right-wingers fit this category. One German right-winger and two far-right Danish politicians describe themselves as sceptical about the claims activists make about the extent of the crisis. It seems clear that the Anglosphere right-wing politicians dominate this category, with their European counterparts tending to populate the next category.

Environmentally sustainable economic thinking

The second group integrate environmental considerations into their approach to the economy and economic policy-making. They make more reference to trade-offs between present and "future generations" than the first group. They believe mitigating climate change should be more of an economic priority than the first group and advocate a greater degree of state intervention to solve it. A key characteristic of this – large – group is their belief that economic policies should promote economic growth that is "environmentally sustainable", and some centre-right politicians have adapted their underlying economic thinking in this way. But this group also include most in the centre and centre left.

Many centrist Democrats are at the more cautious end of this group, with some saying that progressive Democrats are at the more ambitious end, which they usually characterize as meaning being in favour of a greater degree of state intervention. Some centrist Democrats represented coal-mining constituencies, such that their main preoccupation has been with promoting cleaner mining technology or, if they advocate for closing the mines (especially as so many have become unprofitable anyway), promoting the provision of alternative jobs. For instance, a centrist Democrat says that "climate change is urgent", but is concerned about "courageous laid-off coal miners" who "cannot be left behind any longer". Providing jobs cleaning up the disused mines and in renewables would be a win for both the environment and the unemployed. A second Democrat says he started out as an unequivocal liberal (in the overall American sense, rather than as an economic liberal), whose main focus was on "people in need". But now he realizes, "for both pragmatic as well as moral reasons", that "we need a drastic shift in terms of our environmental policy". He wants to give some thought to "subsequent generations".

Also at the more cautious end, a few British Conservatives have incorporated thinking about the environment into their economic policy stance, with one advocating bringing private capital in to complement state spending on environmental policies, through "green bonds". He is unusual in using the term "green transition", which is more common among the French, German and Danish right than the British. One British Conservative who was impressed by Thatcherism in her youth acknowledges how hard it was to renew outdated industries and provide employment in the affected regions, but "hopes" that there are better mechanisms to achieve it now. For these Conservatives, the issue is one of industrial and financial strategy and policy, seemingly bolted on to their usual pro-market approach. However, these Conservatives are far less systematic and consistent than their CDU/CSU counterparts in describing how the environment has shifted their economic thinking at a theoretical level.

The middle part of this group have incorporated the environment into their economic thinking by adapting their goal of "sustainability". This may not necessarily make them act radically on the environment, but it makes their thinking about the environment less of an add-on and more an aspect of their holistic economic approach. The German CDU/CSU, attached to ordoliberal economic thinking, does not see markets as autonomous but as dependent on the state establishing a framework, not just of law but also to ensure a degree of social stability. The notion of "sustainable finance" is core to ordoliberalism: the state should not build up debts that future generations will have to pay and that could cause inflation and, hence, instability. Nearly all the German CDU/

CSU and AfD politicians interviewed have adapted this core notion of sustainability to include "environmental sustainability". They are reflexive enough to acknowledge that this is something they have done only in the last couple of decades, although, noticeably, some do claim to have been trailblazers in this regard as far back as the 1990s. The following examples give a flavour of German right-wing "environmentally sustainable economic policy-making":

> The market economy does not automatically achieve sustainability and environmental goals. Here, too, the state must intervene. So, for me today, bare economic growth is no longer the goal, but I am in favour of qualified economic growth. In other words, economic growth that takes the environment, the fauna, the landscape – nature – into account.

> So, ever since [the 1990s], I do believe there is no contradiction between ecology and economy … In other words, one should not exploit the Earth at the expense of the future. So, this idea of sustainability was for me very important.

Note here how familiar their notion of "sustainability", now incorporating the environment, seems to them, as a natural and effective organizing principle for their thoughts.

I have shown that German politicians raise the environment as an economic issue more often than those of any other country. Germany's reliance on manufacturing industry and coal makes green transition difficult, and they have been grappling with these difficulties for some time. Some represent constituencies in the most industrialized regions of the country. It is striking how in-depth their thinking is, about the balance between the private and public sectors, the role of new technologies and trade-offs between those displaced by greener industries. Getting towards the more radical end of this large second group, one example of German politicians' realism is the stance of German Greens, more moderate in their environmental economics than politicians from environmentalist parties in Denmark, France and the UK. The German Green interviewees say that ten or more years ago they had radical environmentalist policies and considered the economic aspects secondary. However, they have been in coalitions at the Länder level[1] and have made a concerted effort to reach out to voters beyond the usual left environmentalist

---

1. The interviews were conducted before they joined the national government following the 2021 general election.

categories, including those in business. The first Green says, "Radicalism in goal setting is one thing but making it happen is the other thing." As the second Green puts it, the focus is now on what actions governments need to take to achieve the desired "strong green transformation", without dismantling expectations of economic growth. All Greens interviewed explicitly oppose "de-growth" approaches I explore in the next category. As the first Green says, growth is positive, such as a growing baby. The second Green says she would like to put their measured ideas on a sounder theoretical footing. She rejects the heterodox "de-growth" thinking I explore in the next category, but also finds that Keynes, whose broad economic policies she follows, does not address the environment enough to provide an adequate theory of growth; there "really is missing economic ground for this climate question". German Green realism comes out in the notion of accepting some economic dislocation for some workers. The second Green interviewee says they need to "change the complete infrastructure and production processes and so on to get to a … carbon-zero economy". However, to make the green transition in a way that will not damage growth nevertheless means that there will be losers as well as winners. The first Green has been trying to convince consumers that more environmentalist transport could also be more convenient. Like some more right-wing politicians, he emphasizes innovation, some of which will need to come from the private sector. He acknowledges that some workers in the automobile industry will lose their jobs, but he says workers in agriculture lost their jobs in the industrial transition and were forced to retrain. A third Green, an adviser, echoes him, saying: "But I think the most important thing is that we have economic growth without using [up natural] resources … [W]e will still have growth, we still thrive as the economy, *but not every part of it.*"

Some politicians are exploring behavioural economics and how to incentivize through taxation. One LREM politician says, "I am quite convinced that it remains essential to make the economy evolve because economic actors will not change, at least not as fast as it should be done, and it needs to be done." She wants taxation to send a stronger "price signal". But she warns that there must be attention to the regressive nature of some environmental taxation currently aimed at doing this: "We need to build … a progressive system for this environmental taxation that we could imagine for the future."

Most Danish centrists, from the Danish Conservatives on the right to the Social Democrats on the left, fall into this second category, at the more radical end of it. Danish politicians as a whole were in a class of their own compared with politicians from the other countries because of how long their economy and economic policy had been underpinned by environmental concerns. A Red–Green Alliance politician says that "green issues" were adopted by the left very early on. A Socialist People's Party former minister says that "environment, environmental issues and sustainability has been a focus for, I think, numerous years in Denmark", and a Social Democrat politician says that "we are now at a place where green thinking has won" – not a statement made by any interviewees from the other four countries. Denmark's leadership role on environmental economics is demonstrated by the fact that, as long ago as 2007, it set up the Environmental Economic Council alongside the Economic Council. As we have seen in Chapter 5, Danish politicians tend to respect the authority of Danish economists, usually not naming individuals but implying there is a consensus view among them. They say these economists adapted to environmentalism years ago. One Social Democrat says that, when he was a minister, he incorporated environmental costs and benefits into the policy-making process. Rather than resisting, "leading economists in Denmark … inspired the system … and are actually some of the most progressive voices in the climate change debate". Danish Conservatives demonstrate the strength of environmentalist commitment. A former minister says his economic ideas have changed significantly as the climate crisis has escalated. He supports the current ambitious goal of a 70 per cent cut in CO_2 emissions, even if it is "difficult" and "costs a lot of money". Danish companies are now so "advanced" that they can export their solutions and earn money from them, "benefiting the wealth of Danish society and also contributing heavily to reducing the CO_2 emissions globally".

The more radical in this second group mention the need for environmentalist economic policy to also play a part in redistributing wealth. In part this is because they believe in redistribution, and in part because they think it is strategically necessary to gain low-income voters' support for environmentalist policies. But, generally, politicians in the centrist-left parties do not go as far as the "de-growth" supporters in the third category I outline below. The Danish Social Democrat former minister says that voters will be worried that "de-growth" will mean "de-welfare". A French Socialist belongs in this category rather than the third one, because, even though she says that to achieve the "ecological transition" "you need to make sure you have an environmental policy together with fighting inequality hand in hand", she says she does not go as far as to advocate for such "radical green" policies that require her to totally transform how she thinks about the economy.

Socio-ecological restructuring

Politicians in the third category, those believing in "socio-ecological restructuring", are the most radical, because they cannot separate the economy from planetary considerations and they tie environmentalist policies to other necessary radical social changes: "socio-ecological" restructuring, which includes greater gender- and class-based equality. These politicians share a fundamental critique of capitalism.

Some Danish far-left environmentalists who belong in this final category accuse recent Danish governments of moving too slowly. A far-left Danish politician believes they should borrow more for radical state intervention. She foreshadows far-left voices in other countries when she mentions Raworth's "doughnut economy", which re-visions the economy within planetary limits and related to human goals, not consumption. She says:

> I think there is something really interesting happening right now with the doughnut economy. In this theory, there is a limit to resources. So, how can we allocate those resources in the best possible way in our society, in a way where everyone gets something, and it strikes the right balance? It's a pretty exciting way of thinking about economics – without giving an absolute answer on exactly how to do it.

But the fact that she says specific solutions may not be clear-cut reflects the fact that, among those far-left politicians who argue for radical environmentalist economic policies alongside social ones, there is a divide: between those with a Marxist "productivist" and materialistic framework and those who have a more "post-work" orientation and opt for "de-growth".

Productivists

Some German Die Linke politicians are good examples of a more productivist approach. For instance, one advocates radical carbon-taxing and -pricing policies, but argues that German automobile workers still need to have jobs. His solutions to ensuring they can retrain in greener industries focus on structural approaches such as state ownership and enhancing their power through worker democracy. A second Die Linke politician, who has been a leading figure in economic policy-making and alliances across left and far-left and environmentalist groups for many years, explains why he debates the de-growth approach vigorously within the networks but is still opposed to it: "From my point of view, zero growth is nonsense. What is ecologically harmful – that doesn't just have to be zero growth, that has to be reduced ... We also need growth, namely additional services, additional culture, additional education, additional care for the elderly."

In the UK the tensions between the productivist and more de-growth perspectives played out when Jeremy Corbyn was leader of the Labour Party, from 2015 to 2020. One environmentalist Labour politician describes trying to shift the Corbyn leadership's thinking in a more environmentalist direction. The influence of the Marxist productivist trade union element meant that Corbyn's leadership did not consider economic transformation that empowered local communities and was also environmentalist. The votes of key trade union leaders came from the energy sector, in which people were more scared of change; the "interests of the big trade union leaders were in retaining what I consider is yesterday's economics of energy, which is focused around a one-way street from power station to plug". He describes bringing Extinction Rebellion leaders in to speak to the trade unionists, and them being deeply uncomfortable: their "body language was almost seized up; you could see that [Extinction Rebellion activists] were asking them to step outside conventional economic dogmas". He became frustrated that the "productivist" trade union influence and "conventional" left economic thinking prevailed and prevented Corbyn from adopting a more environmentalist position.

> And most of the left really struggled to embrace non-conventional … economics. They just, they just couldn't get their heads around a different scenario, and somehow they – even the best of them – were wanting to run on something on a wing and a prayer. They were hoping that they could rescue the economy from the mess that it was in without abandoning some of the comfort zones of conventional economics that had actually taken us into that mess.

De-growth supporters

It was notable that the British Greens and some Danish far-left politicians believe productivism will not achieve a sufficiently radical solution to the climate change crisis. Not all politicians in this more "de-growth" section of this category subscribe wholeheartedly to the de-growth theories of Nicholas Georgescu-Roegen (1971) and others, that politicians need to stop pursuing growth as a goal and develop a less materialistic base for achieving progress and social well-being. But they at least go as far as questioning materialism, consumerism and how far work is essential to that well-being. They say it is impossible to have a steady "environmentally sustainable" growth rate, and people need to at the least scale down their materialistic desires. A Danish far-left adviser says, "We don't believe that it is a life necessity to have a new iPhone every time a new model comes out. You also don't need the newest computer … We are a consumer society beyond all boundaries, which contributes to our climate problems." A Danish far-left politician says the economy must no longer be "about consumption" and "exponential growth". We have to "rethink" the economy and cannot rely on Marxism, which was from a different time when the climate was not a problem. Economic indicators need to be changed to incorporate the environment and social equality and well-being.

One British Green says the economy "has to fit within the planetary limit", and this is a "physical reality". She says this position is "contested" by most conventional economists, who conceive of the economy as capable of unlimited growth. "Both right and left" try to claim that innovative methods such as carbon capture can solve the environmental crisis, but they have no evidence, particularly for it being a long-term solution. She thinks that conventional economics is the root of the problem, and, as we have seen in Chapter 4, this is one reason they have to reject conventional neoclassical economics and pay attention only to the heterodox. A British Green believes that, even if current economic academic study becomes more pluralist and embraces ecological economics, there will still be resistance for years to come from those trained in the old way of thinking. Her view of the outdatedness of neoclassical economics is echoed by the Corbynite Labour adviser who tried to convert trade unionists, but he is more hopeful, in part because the pandemic is making people more aware of their "interdependencies", that economic thinking will shift eventually: "I think one of the things now, with all the goalposts having been shifted, is that – potentially, at least – we are much more aware of our interdependencies; we have become acutely aware of the basic tenets of interdependent economics." Like many others, he emphasizes a combination of localism in production and employment practices, and strengthened local democracy, so that consumers have control over, for instance, renewable energy production and can clearly see the benefits.

The challenge of communicating

Environmentalist far-left politicians, arguably, have the biggest gap between their own economic visions and those of self-interested voters. A few admit to limiting the range of voters they appeal to. A British Green argues that the aim is to achieve a critical mass, of about 10 per cent of the population, who will then put pressure on the other political parties. There is a general challenge to communicate policies to voters that some interpret as reducing their potential to experience pleasure, in the short term. One French politician describes the "green sober model" as pursuing happiness and purpose through scaling down consumption. He thinks many young people understand that this form of happiness is more important than gratifying immediate pleasures. The "battle" to convince those who believe in the pleasure model will not be won overnight "but we must … we must …; we have to do battle and to stay confident".

Nearly all environmentalist left politicians acknowledge the limited attention voters can pay to economic policy given the pressures on their lives. As a British Green says, there are only a limited number of things she can bring up in an election campaign because of the limited "mental space". Some politicians believe they have a tougher job because their policies are unfamiliar or radical. The same British Green says the idea that economic growth might be damaging is hard to get across.

> We've obviously being saying that for a long time; it's a hard one to get in. I've seen various people try to get it in to interviews, building a bridge across to it, but it's very difficult because the questioner is in a completely different space. I've tried to get people to make programmes about it but it's a real taboo to go there, to say actually maybe economic growth is not such a great thing. They'll pin on a few other measures but they're basically still interested in growth.

Politicians on the left, who are used to targeting low-income voters, are intensely preoccupied with how to win those voters over to more radical environmentalist policies. The challenge is all the harder because these voters are more preoccupied with surviving economically day to day and cannot sustain costs today for the sake of future benefits. In part these politicians have to overcome scepticism about what politicians are capable of doing because of how often low-income voters have been let down in the past. A French Socialist politician describes how the yellow vest protests showed the strength of low- and middle-income opposition to environmentalist measures such as fuel taxes, particularly in rural areas. She says that, before the yellow vest crisis, the ecological question was seen as a "bourgeois" one, "typically raised by vegetarian Parisians eating quinoa". But the protests made her understand what they half knew already, "that the ecological question was a social one, and that it was an issue relating to the poor population instead of the rich one". An American Democrat raises a similar perspective on coal miners, who have been promised many times that they will be retrained for good new jobs. Now the necessity for the mines to close is framed in environmentalist terms, so if the jobs do not materialize it will affect how they see environmentalist policies more broadly:

> But you know we're having trouble in the coalfield today convincing these unemployed coal miners their government is really going to help them. They say: "I want to see it. I don't want to see it ten years

down the road, I want to see it now, because I've been told it for so long and haven't seen it yet." They're not buying it anymore. So that's the problem we have, not only in west Virginia but, I think, in a lot of the heartland of America, of these so-called "smokestack" industries that no longer exist where you have disgruntled workers that feel they're tired of being neglected. And they may buy into climate change. They're not there yet, but they're not ruling it out. They want clean water, they want clean air for their children, as much as anybody on this Earth. But they're not going to suffer putting bread on the table at night to get there anymore.

Conclusion: potential for a settled consensus on the environment?

An economist who has also served in the Trump administration provides valuable insights into where he thinks both economists and the Republican Party are on the economics of mitigating climate change. In his earlier responses he has described how economists working in the administration had a common language, which they did not share with non-economist-trained politicians and bureaucrats. The economists were all neoclassically trained and their common language was based on shared "models and assumptions". This common language meant that the economists could usually reach a consensus. However, he does not think this is so true when it comes to environmental issues. In essence, on the economics of the environment, economists are more split. He describes himself as being far more sceptical than most other economists: "I think economists in the United States are tending more towards the environmental side. I'd say I do not represent the middle of the road on environmental economics in the United States." He thinks the gulf within economists is going to keep widening, because the environment is an issue that requires economists to make projections about the costs of global warming, "which is so outside our level of expertise that it's going to be a source of differentiation". From what he says about Republican politicians, and from what the Republican politicians interviewed say, politicians are less keen to adapt their economic thinking than economists on this issue, and likely to stay in the first categorization of politicians, as being prepared only to make minimal adaptations to their current economic policies.

In Europe, as this chapter shows, a far bigger proportion – in effect, the centre right as well as the centre left – are more united on the need to adapt economic policies to be environmentally "sustainable", with differing degrees of ambition. One French centre-right politician does think that a kind of consensus has been reached. He thinks everyone now shares a belief in applying "sustainability in the ecological domain" and justice between generations to the economy; in the same way that most civilizations have come to believe in equality between the sexes, they will come to believe in equality between the generations.

Within European countries there might be more potential for a settled consensus around this middle way. However, even here, those who believe that such action does not move speedily enough and that there needs to be a more radical socio-ecological transformation will continue to be crucial. Radical environmentalist politicians are, for instance, critical of what they see as a neo-classical perspective on the part of the underambitious economists associated with the Intergovernmental Panel on Climate Change.

The important point is that the kinds of policies politicians talk about to meet climate change targets are what voters see as standard economic policies. Measures to subsidize or tax come down to them, whatever the motive, in the usual economic way: as money going into or out of their pockets. This means that it is hard to separate out an economics of climate change that is distinct in voters' minds from economic policy-making more generally. Therefore, the divergence that underpins politicians' ideas in economics more generally is likely to prevent a consensus on the means to combat climate change, even if a consensus is reached on the aim of reducing climate change. The last word goes to a French Socialist:

> You need to have some idea of economics all the same, to understand the fundamentals, to be interested in the economy, because – even in the green transition today – we have to make that green transition; we don't have a choice ... because, relative to the COP21 objectives, we're just not there. But, nevertheless, we have to master the economy, because we are in a system still where, especially in France, we have a substantial level of social protection, very substantial, perhaps the best in Europe. That social protection – it has to be financed; it has to be financed by economic activity.

To return to the five finance ministers who attended COP26 – a British Conservative, an American Democrat, a German Social Democrat, a Danish Social Democrat and a French centrist – their economic policies to mitigate climate change will be mired in the same considerations as the economic policies they have promoted in the past, because the nature of them is that they will hit voters' pockets. In the same way that parties of the left and right contest what the role of the state in the economy should be, how progressive taxation should be, what acceptable levels of government debt are, they will contest the merits of carbon taxes or renewable energy subsidies.

PART III

Educating voters

At first glance, the national and ideological chapters in Part II have shown stark differences. We go from the deep and taken-for-granted respect of politicians for economists as "scientists" among the centrists of Denmark and the right of Germany to the greater dismissiveness on the part of the Anglosphere right.

There is also an ideological divide, perhaps strongest in the four European countries. The far-left politicians across these countries are experimental, radical and heterodox. They respect some economists, but this is certainly not respect for the authority of economists as a whole, and not in the way that technocrats would see as facilitating any kind of consensus on a settled view. The far left is still wedded to contestation, as one might expect. Far-left politicians also have the greatest challenges when it comes to voters. They are proposing ideas that seem new and require a lot of dedication in time and effort to grasp. They are particularly conscious of how hard it is for them to persuade low-income voters of their environmentalist policies, which, even if they make them as progressive as possible, may nevertheless still provoke fears of potential privations on the part of those who feel let down by past economic policies. On the centre left, respect for economists is partial, since it is almost exclusively applied to Keynesianism. I posed the possibility that the French might be distinctive in their attitude to economists, respecting their plurality, a trend that might spread to other countries, but that would necessitate a wholesale reformulation of the place of economics within the context of expertise. If pluralism proceeds, economics loses its status as a science. This could lead to all sorts of benefits, but it makes it hard to argue for economic technocracy.

With the possible exception of Danish centrists, these chapters in Part II have been united, for different reasons, in pointing out how *unviable* economic technocracy is. They also include undercurrents that show how undesirable economic technocracy would be. The populist threat has varied in its visibility across the five countries, more noticeable in France and the United States. But in this final chapter I argue that relationships with voters more generally are a common problem for the five. The commonality of the problem relates to the morality of politicians' economic visions and their role as elected representatives, and points to a common solution.

9

"Educative" politicians rather than technocracy

> It's up to us to show that every day, in the decisions we take, in what
> we do, that we are for the general interest, that we defend the general
> interest. And, yes, I will tell you that, taking into account all the idi-
> ocies we've committed, we are going to need a bit of time to go up in
> esteem and to find trust again. Voilà.   (French Socialist politician)

The first question I have asked about economic technocracy is whether it is
workable, whether politicians are *likely* to cede more control to economic
experts. Crucial here is their respect for economic expertise. In this chapter,
following the national and ideological variations, I return briefly to the subject
of the low level of that respect overall.

There is more to say here about the second question, of whether economic
technocracy would be *desirable*. I look again, following the national and
ideological variations, at the vexed question of whether economic technocracy undermines democracy. I show that politicians seem uneasy about the
damaging effects on democracy of past attempts they made to take economic
policy out of the political domain and cede control to experts. Their unease
supports the argument that any further embracing of technocracy could fuel
populism and, by doing so, destabilize democracy. However, we need to ask
why politicians were so accepting of the past attempts to take economics out
of the political domain. I return to the long-standing tension, which may pre-
date populism, at the heart of politicians' relationships with voters: the mismatch between politicians' moral economic visions and voters' self-interest.
Politicians have attempted to fudge that mismatch, not only in the past ceding
control to experts but also, more broadly, in the downplaying of explanation
and education in their communication with voters on economic issues. But the
increased complexity of the economic issues, alongside the arrival of populism,

makes it more important than ever before that politicians are more open with voters about their economic visions and make fuller efforts to explain them, reaching the Mansbridge standard of "educative" communication. In the final part of the chapter, I draw on the interviewees who believe they are already educating voters about economics in order to offer their advice as a blueprint for others as to how to educate.

Respect for economic expertise

Even though there is no in-depth coverage of politicians' views of non-economic experts in the book, enough make reference to the difference between economic experts and "hard scientists" to reinforce the argument that their respect for economic experts is generally low. In the case of climate change, they respect the experts on the IPCC who say how rapidly CO_2 has to be reduced to prevent climate change worsening or even how reductions could be best achieved at the hard science level. However, respect for the experts who will propose the economic policies needed to achieve such aims is lower. In this section I conclude, having set out the national and ideological variations in the preceding chapters, that politicians' respect for economic experts is low – certainly lower than for hard scientists – for two reasons. First, politicians' own economic ideas are diverging, and they also see the discipline of economics itself as more divergent. This reduces the potential for respect, on the basis that economists agree on a core consensus in the way that "hard scientists" do, and makes it unlikely that there could ever be cross-party agreement on which economists to cede control to. Second, for politicians in the liberal economics tradition in particular, economics may be becoming less primary.

Diverging ideas at both politician and economist levels

There is a dominant thesis that economic ideas converged significantly in a neoliberal direction within countries, across all Western democracies, from the 1980s. Some empirical scholars, such as Christensen (2017) and Campbell and Pedersen (2014), have challenged this thesis. They argue that there was some convergence but not a uniform "paradigmatic convergence"; neoliberalism remained much more entrenched and influential in the UK and United States than in continental Europe. Politicians in this book, from Germany and Denmark and to a lesser extent France, support the Campbell and Pedersen conclusion of only a *moderate* convergence around neoliberal ideas in continental Europe in the period up to 2008. Nevertheless, they do seem to recognize there was some convergence. The preceding chapters have shown a strong politician perception that since 2008 ideas have diverged again, but we need to assess further whether what they describe is divergence rather than a shift back to the left.

I could draw on politicians' perceptions of how economic ideas have changed only during the period that they were active, which, for most, spanned more than two decades. In every chapter, politicians on the far left seem more confident that since 2008 their ideas have been reaching a larger audience. Some right-wing politicians also complain that this is happening, such as the German right. But I do think on the whole the interviews suggest divergence rather than a shift to the left. In the UK, although the situation remains unclear with Johnsonian Conservatives, there are enough right-wing politicians still confident that free-market solutions are the answer to push back against a notion of a wholesale shift to the left. There is a distinctiveness to the US situation because, although centrist Democrats and centrist Republicans have only minor policy disagreements, the politics is highly partisan, and, as one centrist Democrat explained, the role of the state is a "fundamental" kind of fault line. The progressive Democrats in the United States are portrayed as more radical than previous Democrats in a US context, and this leftward shift in the country is fiercely contested by Republicans, who still have unshakeable free-market beliefs. In the United States both centrist Democrats and Republicans imply that President Trump has further "politicized" the economy. Trump has, in their words, "demagogued" issues such as protectionism, leading to both a less coherent message on the economics and a more contested or political approach to the issue as a whole. Germany and France are still engaged in a contest between left and right, ordoliberal, liberal and Keynesian. This book may even be exaggerating any leftward shift in economic ideas as a result of its under-representation of the far right. But, whereas some of the small number of far-right politicians interviewed have shifted their economic positions strategically and often, as some former UKIP interviewees suggest, the far-right politicians who did agree to interview from Danish and French parties indicate support for the right in the shape of either economic libertarian positions or versions of "economic patriotism". Therefore, the evidence for divergence does seem to be stronger than for a leftward shift.

We should also remember what the politicians have said about the increasingly divergent views of economists themselves. Although just under a half of politicians, mainly on the right, think there is a sense in which economists could be seen as objective, as we progressed through the national chapters it became clearer that the economists in their minds, as they make those judgements, are not the entire discipline; the economists in the "respectful" German right-wingers' minds tend to be ordoliberal only, the economists in the UK and

US right-wingers' minds tend to be "free-market" or "economic liberals", the economists in the Danish centrists' minds tend to be "Scandinavian". Heterodox economists are becoming more influential, and in fact try to break the idea of there being a neoclassical "orthodoxy" that renders them "heterodox" in the first place. Heterodox economists want a recognition that economics is in reality "pluralist". We find that, although some politicians are highly critical of the extent of disunity within economics, others echo this call for a recognition that economics should be seen as more plural and open. But any increased recognition of the plurality of economics raises further hurdles for technocrats, making it more and more difficult for them to claim that economic expertise is equivalent to expertise in epidemiology or hard science.

An interesting point that emerges from these interviews is that politicians from different countries see contesting economic policy in different ways. As many scholars have showed, there is a difference in the political institutions and culture that prevail in coordinated economies in which there are also proportional representation voting systems and traditions of coalition building, such as Denmark and Germany, compared with the more partisan and pluralist democracies of the United Kingdom and United States. In Chapter 5 we find that economic policy appears to be least contested in Denmark out of all the countries, where a social democratic consensus prevails in parties spanning the Conservatives to the Social Democrats. Although Denmark may be able to maintain a less contested economic policy, including drawing on a consensus of respected Danish economists, coming in effect closer to the technocratic ideal, it is hard to imagine that the UK, the United States and France will be able to change their traditions and institutions overnight to become more consensual. These countries are therefore likely to continue to see contested economic policy, possibly increasingly hotly because of the diverging ideas.

Decline in the primacy of economics

There seems to be a particular decline in respect for the neoclassical synthesis among politicians who would traditionally have been associated with liberal economics. French LREM politicians raise the possibility that economic liberals such as themselves are becoming more wary about putting liberal economics first. We may be living through a shift away from the economic liberal emphasis on the primacy of economics (Berman 2006). LREM politicians argue that, in general, politicians are not turning towards new economic thinking so much as being more equivocal about applying economic thinking to problems. The crises one LREM politician cites, of Brexit and Trump's victory, and their own potential populist threat, have made them cautious about liberal economic approaches that pursue economic goals without consideration for social and political responses. This theory that there is a detachment from economic liberalism that contributes to a reduction in the primacy of economics will require further investigation as the coming years unfold.

Many politicians also claim that academic economists, in the sense of being university-based and outside the political fray, are impractical, too abstract and removed from the real world to be useful to them. If they follow economists' advice it is either because the economists are in effect partisan advisers, or, if they are in government, civil servants who have learned to speak their language. One other category of independent economist they often say is useful is "applied" economists: those working on a specific policy, preferably conducted in real-world conditions, that they are interested in. Economist James Galbraith (2021) has recently argued that politicians need more "practical" economists – "scholars who have practical and historical knowledge of the economic problems, policies, and institutions of the world". It is possible that some economists will answer this call, and perhaps a group might emerge who are respected for their pragmatic approach to finding tools to mitigate climate change. But when politicians talk about these "practical" and "applied" economists they are very clear that the advice they offer is limited and does not have the potential expansiveness of an overall economics "approach", such as Keynesianism. They would be very much in control of the process whereby they consulted them; they would have set the goals and general policy direction before they consulted them on the detail.

How economic technocracy undermines representative democracy

The second barrier to economic technocracy is that the politicians in this study believe that it will undermine representative democracy. Just as this book focuses on economic technocracy alone, it also focuses on five stable democracies, so this judgement is perhaps not applicable to democracies with higher levels of corruption or reputations for incompetent government. But, whether implicitly or explicitly, and across the political spectrum, I argue that these politicians are uneasy about the prospect of technocracy provoking a backlash from voters who feel they have been shut out from an area of decision-making that they see as crucial to them.

In an otherwise detailed and well-balanced consideration of whether technocracy is "friend" or "foe" of representative democracy, Eri Bertsou (2020: 267) raises the question of whether technocracy from the 1980s onwards should be "held responsible" for the rise of populism in European and American democracies, by causing an angry backlash. But her main answer is that perhaps demands for technocracy might increase again after a populist phase, as if there is a kind of natural swing of the pendulum between the two states of populism and technocracy at extremes, with democracy in the middle. This argument does not answer the case about whether technocracy *causes* a populist backlash. Ignacio Sánchez-Cuenca (2020: 60) suggests that technocracy may undermine what he describes as the "depth" of democracy by hollowing it out. He means this in the sense that, in the past, control was ceded to neoliberal economists, who reduce democracy's depth by taking areas of economic policy out of the political domain or out of elected politicians' hands. However, there is another sense in which technocracy may undermine the depth of democracy: by making it less stable. The technocrat vision of a naturally swinging pendulum that corrects democracy's failures, by going in a technocrat direction when democracy becomes over-responsive and in a populist direction when it becomes over-responsible, risks reducing the chances of the pendulum ever resting in the democracy sweet spot. The swinging pendulum is a less desirable state than stable representative democracy.

Politicians' views on how beneficial or damaging the effects of handing over control of economic policy in the past have been are complex but revealing in this respect. Most scholars argue convincingly that politicians in all five countries did, from the 1980s onwards, give up some of their control of economic policy to experts. They granted independence to central banks, giving up some control over monetary policy. They ceded some of their control over fiscal and industrial policy to technocratic bodies at arm's length from the political arena (Burnham 2001; Fawcett *et al.* 2017). In Caroline Kuzemko's (2014) assessment of this process in the case of UK energy policy, during the 1980s and 1990s privatizations, she argues that there were two negative effects over time that undermined the depth of democracy. First, "*political* deliberation about energy" declined (Kuzemko 2014: 112), so there was less discussion between politicians about what path to take. Second, the technocrats modelled energy systems, but in such technical language that generalist politicians and voters disengaged from learning about or talking about energy policy. She, along with other scholars such as Peter Burnham (2001), highlight politicians' motives in giving up control. Although some genuinely believe the technocrats will run energy more effectively, they also believe that reducing their accountability for energy policy will reduce the potential for voters, who can never understand the full complexities and technicalities, to blame them for any failures.

A former UKIP politician reinforces the case that depoliticization made voters feel pushed out by the established parties, leading them to turn to parties such as his own. He explains how removing key policy areas from the political arena enabled that: voters were angry because they felt they had experienced years of not being "consulted" by politicians. They had a sense that big changes were happening and that the politicians making these decisions were deliberately not consulting them, or were not telling them the whole truth, the example he gives of the latter being estimates of the number of people from the rest of the European Union who would come to work in Britain following the 2004 expansion of EU membership. The UKIP politician believes the voter anger was not so much "that policy X was good or bad" as "that they had just been ignored". He describes voters as having been "deferential" in the sense of acquiescent during much of the depoliticizing neoliberal era and then suddenly deciding they had had enough.

I have said that politicians' unease about past depoliticization is implicit as well as explicit. On the right, relatively few interviewees proactively raise how far they have given up control over a range of economic policies. One reason may be that they see it as having been an inevitable and settled process. Key elements, such as independent central banks and EU-level institutions, would be impossible to undo. But another possible reason is a kind of complicity in how convenient it was to quietly cede control. If that is the case, we should question what politicians say about being unwilling to give up more control in the future. Even in these confidential interviews they might be *claiming* to be wanting to stay in control, because it would be embarrassing to admit they thought elected politicians could not cope.

To explore this question further, of how far politicians might privately want to give up control, politicians' responses to one question about what they think voters expect from them in economic policy are illuminating. I asked, "Do you think voters underestimate or overestimate what you can do?" A few, usually on the left, find their voters *under*estimate what politicians can do, have come to expect very little and have "given up". A German Die Linke politician says:

> I'm even afraid that among the people who are now more likely to vote Die Linke, because they would like more social security and more security in their own right, and are in more precarious positions, that such a defeatist attitude – "You can't change a lot anyway" – is even more prevalent. I can't back it up with any numbers; it's an everyday experience that I have in conversations.

A British Labour politician describes how "there's swathes of people who don't care and think [politics] is an irrelevance"; they say that "what you do is a complete irrelevance". For politicians on the far left in particular, the problem is that past depoliticization may have contributed to this perspective that politicians cannot deliver policies in their interests, let alone the general interest. Some pin their hopes on the effects of the pandemic, arguing that the increase in state intervention may have increased voter expectations about what politicians can achieve economically in future.

However, on balance, most interviewees, whether from left or right and across the countries, say voters still *over*estimate what politicians can achieve in economic policy (with a subgroup saying they both under- and overestimate). A British Labour politician says, "I think [voters] massively overestimate." They often go on to qualify this point by saying that the situation is unhealthy and leads to voter distrust. Many offer the view that politicians and voters play a kind of game. A German CDU/CSU politician says, "When I read some of the party programmes, including my own, it is of course also a bit of marketing, that is part of it ... Then I have the impression that the influence is estimated too high." A British Conservative agrees:

> It's a very difficult question, this, because I think deep down a lot of [voters] know that a government's room for action and manoeuvre is quite constrained, and more constrained than it ever admits during a general election. And the electorate and the main political parties have an ... unhealthy pact that we'll all kind of kid ourselves that we can do all these amazing things that we talk about during a general election and ... and then there's sort of disappointment all round.

Interviewees say that, as politicians, they cannot admit to not controlling economic policy to voters. A French centre-right politician says the problem is that "any politician who might be elected is obliged to say that he has some power". The politician believes the "scientific and academic truth" is that "the trends are global", and politicians cannot change much, but politicians who say this to voters will not get elected. He sees it as a profound problem with the democratic system that it leads "to this untruthful role" for politicians. It fuels populism, because populist politicians also claim to be able to solve economic problems that are in reality impossible to solve.

Therefore, I did not find support for the general thesis that has been dominant in the past: that it is mainly the left that opposes depoliticization, taking economic policy out of the political domain. It seems to me that the right shares some of the same unease with the left about the damage that can be done by taking economics out of the political arena. The fact that a majority of politicians tend to think that voters have not scaled down their expectations of what politicians are capable of doing in the economic arena suggests that, even if, privately, they acknowledge that one reason for past depoliticization was to absolve politicians from blame, they do not think that strategy has worked, and in fact it has brought new problems in the shape of rising confusion and distrust. For this reason, I think we should take interviewees' claims at face value when they say that they do not want to give up further areas of economic policy to experts.

Education: why politicians need to be the ones to do it

Given that economic technocracy is not workable or desirable, the only option for politicians who want to increase the stability and depth of democracy is to engage more actively with voters on economic issues, not hiding behind expertise but setting out openly how contested economic issues are. In other words, politicians seeking support for what they believe are responsible economic goals must "educate" voters. First I show why it has to be the politicians who do the educating and not other actors.

Politicians dismiss the ability of economists and the media to educate voters. Unsurprisingly, given their often expressed judgement on economists as overly theoretical and technical, and prone to abstraction, no politicians suggest that economists can educate voters effectively. When they proactively raise economists in this context, it is to explicitly dismiss this possibility. A French leftist politician says that economists "are very badly understood by" voters. The second group whose educative skills politicians dismiss are the media. There is no direct question about the media, and surprisingly few politicians raise it at any point of their interview. A few directly accuse the media of misinforming. A US Republican claims that, in his opinion, voters do not get adequate explanations from the media. When the media are their only source of information, he says that "I think the understanding is limited". The interviewees sometimes raise voters' reliance on superficial outlets for news. It is significant that only a couple raise the possibility of the media playing a constructive role, and, even then, they are grudging. For instance, a French Socialist says the real challenge for politicians is answering the question "What is the relationship between citizens and information?". She thinks it is "up in the air" as to whether "economic journalists" will be able to play a role in providing high-quality information.

Teachers fare better. About one-quarter of the interviewees advocate schools playing more of a role in economics education. Most of these are in the four European countries and come from the right. For instance, a French centre-right politician would like secondary school pupils to study economics, because "there's a huge deficit in the explanation of the economy". In some cases the politician concerned has worked out the programme in some detail: that it should be an hour a week from the mid-teens, or that it should involve trips to companies rather than just being classroom-based. The economic education curriculum that they advocate is about the wider economy and not just personal finances. However, often these are the same politicians who have criticized the leftist leanings of teachers who, they say, know very little about economics, so this is a barrier to the effectiveness of school-based economics education. The lack of support for economics education from outside this relatively small group on the right reflects how difficult it would be to promote economics education at school level without provoking controversy.

A few, including some from the left, call for a different subject of voter education: civics. Civics would take place at school level and be reinforced for adult voters, and would make the politicians' job of explaining how they decide economic policies easier. One US Democrat explains how she has constantly maintained civics education with her voters, who were "a fairly educated electorate" but still had only limited understanding of how the legislative system worked. She "spent a lot of time trying to educate voters about how the process really works", through town hall meetings, among other methods.

Even if there was intensive economic education at the school level in all five countries, there are three reasons politicians would need to supplement it, with their unique perspective. First, they communicate with voters face to face on a more equal footing than any other political actors. As they say over and over again in their interviews, they talk to their constituents, from a wide range of social backgrounds, on a daily basis. There is also a kind of contractual and mutual dependence between politicians and voters, in the sense that voters know they have some power over them. As many of the US politicians stress, a huge part of their job is "campaigning". As we have seen in previous chapters, they develop skills in translating data into "stories" for voters.

Second, education is one of the ways in which they can restore citizen trust in them. Many raise the issue of how much they have to rebuild trust, particularly in the Anglosphere and France. A Democrat politician from a coal-mining district believes President Trump degraded economic messaging. But he believes one reason voters were susceptible to Trump's simple economic messages was that politicians had promised too much in the past. He draws the lesson that, in order to rebuild that trust, politicians have to be "transparent with these individuals", involving them in the process.

A French Socialist who has been exercised about the effects of shutting voters out from economic debate during the neoliberal decades, which she thinks has eroded trust, argues that they need to be brought back in. She says it will take skill to convince them it is worth re-engaging. She tries to have "an educational approach" to the economic question. The first task is to stop voters saying to themselves that economic issues are "too complicated". She thinks this leads to confusion and demoralization for the citizen, who starts to see the economy as "obscure, grey, something which hinders and something which is serious". She adds that they are more convinced of their knowledge on things such as Covid-19 and the pandemic than their views about economics. This is because the neoliberal decades and narrative that nothing could be done to counteract market forces taught them that "the economic question is not a matter on which they have the right to have an opinion". They feel that they are caught in a paradox, "where, on one side, they feel that the economy is a major and decisive matter but, on the other, they don't feel authorized to … say what they think". As it was politicians who aggravated this paradox, she thinks it needs to be politicians who encourage voters to feel they have enough economic knowledge to re-engage.

Finally, because economic issues are in reality contested, it has to be the agents of contestation who explain that to voters. Teachers and so on might be able to teach some nuts and bolts, or critical faculties, but politicians are the ones best placed to explain to voters how and why their policies differ from those of other parties.

A blueprint for "educating": "it could have been worse"

In the previous chapters I have drawn on Jane Mansbridge's advocacy for more politicians to aim for the highest standard in persuading voters, one that is based on "explaining" and "clarifying" (Mansbridge 2003: 525–6), to which she gives the encompassing term of "educating" (Mansbridge 2003: 519). However, we need to draw on the politicians' accounts in this book to elaborate on what her "educative" standard should look like in practice.

Drawing on Mansbridge's work, Lisa Disch (2011: 101) says that a first necessary condition for the educative standard is that the politician does not intend to manipulate or deceive. A crucial component of not intending to manipulate is that politicians are honest about how moral their own economic visions are. Throughout the book we have found that, whether they are from the left, the Christian Democrat right or even American Republicans, many politicians talk about moral economic visions – of distributive justice, or of stability combined with free markets – that drove them into politics. They are able to discuss these economic ideas enthusiastically in interviews. However, when asked how they think voters see the economy, almost every one gives the answer "Through the lens of their own well-being". They see voter self-interest as natural. How, then, do they resolve such a fundamental mismatch? The vast majority imply that, whenever possible, they address the voters' self-interested concerns rather than expounding on their reasons for supporting free trade, or subsidy or the degree of distributive justice they aim for. This shyness about the morality of their economic visions is a kind of deception that, by omission, degrades the quality of the debate.

Relatedly, politicians will not be able to explain and clarify if they do not raise the profile of their economic ideas relative to easier-to-understand cultural ideas. Some criticize populist politicians as ignoring economic discourse completely, or producing messages that distort. But, even if they make some greater mention of economic policy than the populists, they do not do it in enough depth.

So, if politicians are the ones who have to do the educating, what blueprint can any of the politicians in this book offer for others to follow? Our interviewees suggest that a balance needs to be struck between "starting where the voter is" and "appealing to voters' intelligence".

"Starting where the voter is"

In attempting to educate, which Disch (2011: 101) says includes "clarifying" terms used, the politician faces the challenge of starting where the voter is, hooking onto his or her daily experience. Politicians give many examples of "starting where voters are". A Green politician who campaigns for more environmentalism says, "If you are trying to make the public case ... you are going to have to start from where they are." An American Democrat says she explained her support for a key industry in terms that directly affected her constituents' lives, so that they would understand: "Oh, that really is important to the economy." Some use food analogies, such as the French Socialist comparing banks that had made bad investments in the run-up to 2008 to putting rotten eggs in a salad. Many British politicians refer to Margaret Thatcher's skill in using everyday language and images, such as choosing apples in a grocer's shop. Even a Labour politician says she struck a chord with many people in the 1970s by saying " 'Look at the effects of inflation.' And people could see it when they went to the shops; what they bought one week was costing a lot more next time." The lesson a Conservative draws from this is also that "the politician has to persuade people [that] you care about them". Some simply explain using as plain language as possible. A US Democrat tried to get support for excluding homes from assets when people went bankrupt: "And I explained that in just really common-sense terms to people as I was going around the congressional district. And I would say to them, 'The one thing that I'm going to work on as soon as I get into Congress is fixing that part of the bankruptcy code, so that you can keep your home.' And it makes perfect sense to people."

A Danish Social Democrat says that, regarding the green transition, she uses simple examples concerning bus availability. One far-left German politician describes using the example of Lake Constance to make voters believe that environmental improvements are possible:

When I sometimes hear in the left spectrum that it's capitalism, you can't change anything, then I can only say … well, once before Lake Constance was about to tip over, and we heard that one couldn't do anything in the Ruhr and Rhine – and today everything is clean. So back then it was about CFCs, and then we got it under control. This is exactly how you can get the CO_2 question under control if you want to.

One Republican describes visiting factories to persuade workers to support some of Trump's tax policies. By visiting the factory, he literally "starts where they are". I repeat his script in some detail to show how he used question and answer, each time starting with where he thought they were to build up the levels of understanding:

> Well, I would go and I would meet with the leadership of the company, and then I would tour the factory floor, and then I would do a question and answer with the employees. And it was so interesting to me, because, you know, in one case I got a group of employees together – 50 in a lunchroom – and, you know, they're not really happy to be hearing from me … Even though they're not working now, it's like "What is this guy? I'm not really interested." And I totally got the joke. So I said, "Look, how many of you would be pleased – just give me a show of hands – how many of you would be pleased if the company brought back money that it was investing overseas right now and it brought that back here in this facility and extended an assembly line? Raise your hand if you're for that." And, of course, every hand goes up. I said, "OK, so what you're telling me is you are for what's known as repatriation. You're for it. And I'm for it too. Now, let me tell you what it is and how it works … What do we have to do to incentivize your boss or incentivize the company to invest here? Well, when they bring their money back that they've earned overseas, we want it to be as small a taxable event as possible." And people go, "Yeah, that's right." So, boom, OK, now you're talking.

Some have used evocative and everyday objects, such as Hershey Kisses. A passionate free-trade Republican represented a district where many voters believed that manufacturing plans had closed down as a result of competition from China and were gravitating to support Trump protectionism as a solution, believing tariffs would make Chinese imports more expensive and boost demand for home-produced goods. He found that, however damaging, an upside of Trump actually introducing some tariffs on steel and aluminium was that he was able to use them as an effective "educational tool".

I said, "Let me explain to you the aluminium tariffs." And I represented [a district] where they make a lot of chocolate, a lot of candy.
And I pointed out, "You know protectionism? OK, let's see. Cocoa: we
don't grow it in North America, we must import it. Now, what would a
tariff do there? It would be a problem. And they use a lot of sugar." […]
I said, "This is what protectionism does: your sugar costs are higher."
On aluminium tariffs, I said, "Oh, by the way, all those Hershey Kisses
that they make (they make 70 million a day at that plant, all wrapped
in a very fine aluminium foil) and – guess what? The packaging prices
are just going up now. And you worry why these companies move their
production facilities to Canada and Mexico? Well, it's not because of
labour prices; it's because of sugar prices. And, if you do aluminium
tariffs – guess what? It might be [they move] because of packaging
costs. So, maybe, we all need to think about this a little differently.

Those who opposed Thatcher's preoccupation with bringing inflation
down, or Trump's repatriation tax reform, may argue that in these examples there are unacceptable simplifications or distortions. However, I argue
that these politicians, as long as they also did the civic job of teaching what
politicians can and cannot do, are at least attempting to engage and draw
out voters on economic issues, starting from where they are. Relatedly, the
politicians who claim to engage voters effectively say that a final key component in "starting where voters are" is not patronizing them. A politician who
stresses the "don't patronize" theme is a US Democrat who wants to persuade
voters to support more environmentalist policies but does not think a punitive or judgemental tone is constructive. He says Democrats will not make
progress by saying to voters " 'We're going to do everything we can to screw
you for driving the cars. And, by the way, I'm going to shame you, make you
feel bad about whatever – you know, the economy, the environment, equal
rights. It's all your fault, because you made bad choices.' " He says such a hec-
toring approach just makes voters angry. They might not tell the politician
they are angry but they then go out and "vote for Donald Trump".

"Appealing to voters' intelligence"

However, as well as starting where people are, politicians also have to appeal
to voters' intelligence, without simplifying so much that they fail to raise
their level of understanding with regard to what are usually complex issues.
A French Socialist warns that the simple-to-understand issues may not always
be the most important issues:

I am very struck, if you want, by the fact that we often take very small steps … An example: we talk about the environment through plastic. And most people will say, "You see, we need to ban plastic straws." Great. That's what we've done, or, in any case, what we are ready to do. I don't think that's going to change the ecological equilibrium of the planet. I think questions of vehicles, mobility, energy, travel, of their carbon emissions – that's much more important than banning plastic straws.

The difficulty of striking the right balance is one reason why he says politicians need much help and instruction in how to communicate.

A second French Socialist says the solution to the problem of voters expecting too much and being disappointed, compounding rising distrust in politics, is one of education. Currently what voters feel is "a deep scepticism" about what politicians can achieve. But politicians have encouraged this by "failing to call … on people's intelligence to try to understand what we're trying to do". He says that politicians should always "have to appeal to intelligence, not to the lowest emotions of your supporters or of those around you". As soon as politicians get in the habit of appealing to lower emotions, they lose the capacity to appeal to intelligence: "Then, basically, people no longer want to think through 'but it could have been worse; but this decision nevertheless had a positive effect; but, well, etcetera.'" He counsels against "oversimplification" as lowering the level of debate so that populists find it easier. He wants voters to think through hypothetical scenarios in order to arrive at the more "it could have been worse" kinds of qualified judgements. Politicians should speak more honestly to voters. They should also counter despair with concrete examples showing that some things *have* been achieved.

Some politicians actually run lectures or courses in schools, colleges and community groups to appeal to and cultivate voters' intelligence. A German right-wing politician has developed a game in which market procurement or business claims are simulated so as to teach young people about the "market economy order". A German far-left politician runs workshops for voters, so he is obviously only reaching those already keen to be educated. But he describes how "some of the people called home on the first evening, and on the second evening to say to their partners, 'We have to rethink everything. Everything we have thought so far is completely, completely wrong. We don't have too high wages and the Japanese won't overrun us and the Chinese or anything … all very different.'"

We have already seen that politicians value their ability to translate economic messages into "stories". However, "data" can be turned into stories that may at some level hook onto emotions but also aim to appeal to "intelligence".

A far-right Danish politician who produces videos says he uses "a lot of concrete examples of what actually the government is spending their money on … and I put it out there to people; I don't conclude for them. And I think that's one of the reasons that I have quite a fair amount of success right now."

The pandemic may help politicians to appeal more to voters' intelligence. I conducted these interviews at the height of the 2020–21 period, when lockdowns were novel and no one was yet vaccinated, through to times when there was great weariness with the debate about whether lockdowns should be lifted. Although many countries included large swathes of their populations who were not listening to official spokespeople, there is evidence from Reuters (Newman 2020) that the pandemic forced a larger proportion of the public than usual to pay consistent attention to a complex and fast-moving phenomenon. Many politicians, whether left or right, believed the pandemic would also engage voters by making them think that governments could take decisive actions after all, which increases the incentive for them to listen to politicians' explanations. But even those right-wing politicians who hoped that support for increased state intervention would not be permanent, and things would return to normal, recognized the closeness of voter attention to news during the pandemic.

Conclusion

I began this book with the heaviness of the burden on the finance ministers – a US Democrat, British Conservative, French centrist, German Social Democrat and Danish Social Democrat – working out how to meet the targets agreed at COP26. It may be that politicians are disingenuous, that despite their dismissal of economic experts up until now they have relied on them and do value them more than they care to admit. In that case, they might be tempted to give up more control in future, to "depoliticize" the economics of the environment. But they will endanger democracy in the process. The fact that the new technocracy many call for to mitigate climate change is one that they hope will be staffed by more "progressive" economic experts than in the past will not alter voter perceptions about being shut out. Voters will experience economic policies to mitigate climate change in the same way that they experience all economic policies: as affecting their taxes, job prospects and incomes. They have to be given a say.

The most powerful insight into politicians that this study offers is their unease about any further ceding of power to economic experts, however tempting it might seem. They have ducked away from talking in enough detail about their economic visions for a long time. But they have been shaken by the populist manifestations of the last five years: Brexit; Trump; the rise of the AfD, the RN and the yellow vests. They have only one choice: to re-engage with voters on economic issues, in a contested form, in the political domain, and attempt to win them over to whatever version of responsible economic policy it is that they believe in. Concerned citizens should not give up on elected politicians, but urge them to make every effort to engage voters in two-way and educative economic debate.

APPENDIX

Research design and methods

My overall aim was to research politicians' economic ideas inductively, in order to describe them accurately, being relatively open about the main themes that would emerge, following an interpretivist epistemological approach (Bevir & Rhodes 2003; Cramer 2016). This book is based on the dominant themes that emerged from in-depth, semi-structured interviews with 85 elected politicians and 14 political advisers from the UK, France, Germany, Denmark and the United States. The interviews were conducted primarily by video conference, between February 2020 and December 2022.

I was responsible for the "politician strand" of a broader project exploring economic thinking. It was based in the Politics Department at University College London. I have used the first-person singular, "I", throughout the book to reflect my responsibility for much of the research design, and for the data collection and analysis. However, as I acknowledge in the preface, the wider research team had already made some decisions, helped me make others and contributed to some of the interviewing. Therefore, in this appendix I use a mix of "I" and "we" as appropriate. I set out details about our case selection, choice of interview as method, interview design, analysis, recruitment strategy and characteristics of those interviewed.

Case selection

The research team chose Germany, France, Denmark, the UK and United States to research for two reasons. First, they are long-established democracies with varying institutional traditions in degrees of federalism, separation of powers and voting systems. Second, they have relatively well-functioning economies and some autonomy over their economic policies. They correspond both to "varieties of capitalism" (Hall & Soskice 2001), ranging across coordinated to liberal and Scandinavian categories, and to growth models (Baccaro & Pontusson 2016), ranging across consumption and export-led categories. However, as I stress in Chapter 1, the primary aim is not to focus on how different economies and political traditions may affect politicians' economic thinking, but to *describe* their attitudes to economists and voters.

Why interview politicians?

The research team has heeded the call for descriptive studies of ideas to "primarily rely on direct evidence of policy actors' ideas and belief" (Daigneault 2014: 463). Politicians' economic ideas at the general level have been neglected. There is rich and detailed evidence on how economists attempt to influence politicians (Campbell & Pedersen 2014; Christensen 2017), but direct investigation of the more general economic understandings of elected politicians is lacking, despite the important part they play in the policy-making process. Similarly, there is extensive study of voters' economic attitudes, but not of politicians' *perceptions* of voters' attitudes, which may act as a constraint on their policy-making.

There are empirical studies based on analysing politicians' written and publicly spoken accounts, such as Stephanie Mudge's (2018) study of social democrats' economic thinking. There are also numerous analyses of politicians' thinking on specific economic policies, such as tax (for example, Kemmerling 2017; Carstensen & Röper 2019), and rich ethnographic work centring on politicians' relationships with their constituents or work on a particular committee (Fenno 1966, 1973). However, we thought there would be value in conducting interviews whose aim was to explore

- politicians' economic ideas at the general level;
- politicians' perceptions of the degree of influence of economists on those general ideas; and
- politicians' perceptions of how voters think about the economy.

We chose to interview because interviews allow the politicians to speak for themselves, without the imposition of the researcher's preconceptions about the kinds of approach they will take to economic thinking. They enable us to gather rich data from a relatively large number of people in the time and budget we had available. From a practical point of view, we also believed it likely that politicians would be more likely to respond to requests for an interesting and reflective conversation than to any request for more quantitatively oriented data collection, such as a survey.

By specifying that the interviews would be confidential, we hoped politicians would speak more openly and honestly than when justifying their ideas for the public record. Talking to politicians confidentially allows us to investigate uncertainty and variability in their ideas, which tend to be downplayed in public political speech. The main limitation of this interview-based approach, as opposed to one grounded in observed behaviour, is that politicians may misrepresent important parts of their own thinking, even in private. Here we do not suspect deliberate deception but, rather, that three more subtle factors may be at play. First, our position as researchers conducting the interviews may induce a certain type of answer that the politicians think that we are looking for. In terms of deference to economic expertise, we are in an ambiguous position. As political scientists, some politicians interpreted us as being very much outside that category of experts, but others saw us as bearers of the very economic authority – and, in particular, academic economic authority – that we were asking about. However, the general direction of influence here is clear: this identification should have led our interviewees to be more positive about the authority of economists and the utility of their way of thinking. Over-adherence to this position did not seem to be a widespread problem among the interviewees, who were generally quite willing to be critical of economists. Second, some scholars highlight that political elites are accustomed to more overtly critical scrutiny – from journalists – in the interview format, leading them to see an interview as calling for justifications of what they do (Harvey 2011). The confidential status of our interviews is intended to guard against this perception, and we were careful to emphasize that we were interested in our interviewees' thoughts and perspectives, in their own words. Equally, the nature of the questions – open-ended and descriptive – should work against this tendency. However, the need to self-justify may remain as an impetus to interviewees potentially overstating their own personal roles, including their independence from economists. The more general psychological tendency to self-enhancement may lead politicians, in interviews, to overstate their roles and their positive attributes (Sedikides & Gregg 2008). However, a gap between politicians' perception of themselves and a more objective evaluation of their influence is the price of any design that relies directly on the perspectives of those involved, not just interview accounts. Wherever relevant I have highlighted where exaggeration might have been taking place.

Finally, and more generally than simply overstating their own positive traits and influence, it may be that our interviewees are not very effective analysts of their own thought processes. The influences on their approach to economic policy-making might not be transparent to them. The difficulty of accurate self-description is more general: the mistake might be in any number of directions. Again, to the extent that this discrepancy exists, it is nevertheless interesting to discover; if politicians believe economists to be useless, yet nevertheless follow their prescriptions, this tells us that economic influence works differently from if they pursue uneconomic approaches yet laud the importance of economists' analyses. But this remains an important caveat to bear in mind in interpreting the findings.

How generalizable are findings emerging from this particular window in time, much of which overlapped with the Covid-19 pandemic? On the one hand, they are temporally specific. On the other hand, although I did ask one direct question about how far they thought the pandemic would affect their economic thinking and voters' economic thinking, the interviewees do not bring the pandemic into their answers as much as might be expected. The most common time reference they make is to the period since the 2008 financial crisis. I am tentative about claiming that these interviews provide evidence about how much has changed over time, because there is no similar previous study to compare with. However, I do believe it is important to document politicians' assessments of changes over time. As the demographic details will show, their age profile was heavily weighted in the 50-plus direction, and even politicians in their early 40s had much to say about how their ideas had changed, or how changing economic conditions had prompted them to question economists or economic thinking, particularly from the 2008 financial crisis onwards.

In the rest of this appendix, for the sake of clarity and to reflect the inductive nature of the research process, I describe it chronologically.

Interview design

I developed and tested the interview guide in pilot interviews. The interview guide consisted of a set of common questions that were general enough to ask politicians from different countries and parties, with and without experience in government. They consisted of three stages to reflect our three research aims. A first autobiographical section included a consistent warm-up question asking politicians to describe when they had been most involved with economic issues during their careers. We then asked about the sources of their economic ideas, and their evolution over time. The second part of the interview focused on the nature of their current ideas and the utility of economic expertise. A final section consisted of questions about perceptions of voters' thinking about the economy.

I used a semi-structured interview format. The questions were worded in an open-ended way, such as "How do you think voters see the economy?" I used "economic ideas" as a sensitizing concept (Blumer 1954) in the data collection and initial analysis. For instance, the subject strap line in the interview email was "Politicians' economic ideas". The questions were nearly all about "economic ideas". I found that politicians naturally interpreted economic ideas to be quite general, at the abstract level, often using a word such as "goal" for them. They used policies as examples to illustrate this more general level of thinking. I asked one direct question to try to assess the normativity of their ideas, which asked them whether they distinguished between economic ideas and "values". We tried to stick to broadly similar phrasing and ordering of questioning throughout all the interviews.

The interviews lasted an average of one hour. The aim was to encourage the interviewee to talk at length with minimal interruptions in the shape of prompt or probe questions. This is not an approach that would have been productive with all types of professions, but politicians mostly responded enthusiastically to the chance to talk at length. Curiously, despite the number of interruptions I have been used to in past face-to-face interviews with politicians, these online interviews were not interrupted often; just a few phone calls from journalists. The interviews nearly always ended on a positive note, and most politicians indicated that they had found them interesting and that they had given them the chance to reflect. We conducted the interviews in either English or the home language, at the choice of the interviewee. They were recorded, and transcribed and – when necessary – translated, by the wider research team.

Analysis

The analysis proceeded as follows. I analysed the interviews without preconceived, pre-defined categories for coding using an inductive and iterative thematic approach (Braun & Clarke 2006, 2013). I was looking for variation and commonality in both latent and surface meaning. Thematic analysis involves open coding, often developing several hundred codes in the first instance. Examples of codes I identified are "Voters are self-interested", "Source economic ideas childhood experience", "Economists not useful because practical". Sometimes the same text got coded two or three different ways. Sometimes the text was a few words, sometimes a whole paragraph. I then refined and grouped the codes into themes. In subsequent stages of the analysis I refined the codes and themes further. In thematic analysis it is important not to read interviews in groups, as this may distort how the researcher judges patterns. So I read the interviews in many different orders: chronological; alphabetical; and based on country and ideology. I read the interviews many, many times.

In the earlier stages of analysis I focused on variation in the *content* of ideas, such as references to growth, prosperity or environmental sustainability.

The aim here was to note patterns across the ideological groupings and to contextualize other aspects of their economic thinking. In the later stages of analysis I focused on beliefs about how their ideas had developed and how far they were influenced by economists. I focused on their answers to questions about how they thought voters saw the economy and about their notions of the role of the politician. These themes were the most dominant themes. It was impossible to analyses all potential themes in the time available or in a way that would provide a coherent account. For instance, I have neglected in this book what they said about the impact of the pandemic, because their thoughts about it were less developed, more tentative, generally less interesting than their thoughts about the other issues. I have also not analysed in depth some of the patterns on ideology, such as the differing language used, for instance, by centre-left politicians across the five countries to describe equality aims.

Although I was knowledgeable about scholarship on economist influence, representative democracy and technocracy before conducting this research, the inductive nature of the process as a whole meant that I did not decide how to frame the evidence in the book until after I was part way through the analysis. Before I started I did not know quite how starkly the theme of a con-flict between responsibility and responsiveness would be revealed. Because the interviews were so revealing on the subject of expertise as well, I went back to the literature on representative democracy and technocracy to gauge how far the politicians' views seemed to support it.

As with any research design, this one had weaknesses. I have tried to be transparent in the preceding chapters about where I was getting answers to direct questions that pertain to economists, such as "How useful do you find them?", and where I was extrapolating from the other questions to provide extra insights into their attitudes to economists. Having done the analysis of the open-ended interview guides I designed, I can say that, if I had my time again, I might design a different interview more closely targeted on that key issue of attitudes to economists. But I am nevertheless confident that there is also validity in designing a more open and broad-ranging interview and seeing what dominant themes emerge.

Recruitment strategy and interviewee characteristics

I decided to focus on elected politicians who are close to economic decision-making, rather than elected politicians in general. If I had interviewed poli-ticians in general this book would have been very different. The advantage of interviewing only politicians interested in economics is that they give deep and rich answers and are the politicians closest to actual economic decision-making. As some of these interviewees pointed out, they have colleagues who may pay attention to bread-and-butter economic issues at election time but whose daily attention throughout their political careers has been on other areas, such as foreign policy or human rights. This perception by "economic" politicians of many of their colleagues as "non-economic" was weakest in the UK, where there was more support for "generalism", arguably reflected in the somewhat weaker committee system and more fluid movement between ministerial departments.

As interviewing is so labour-intensive, I had to limit the number of total interviewees to around 20 in each country, slightly fewer in the smaller country of Denmark. In each country I aimed to recruit across the ideological spectrum. I limited the sample to parties with national representation either at the national parliament or European Parliament level. The reason for including some MEPs was, in part, to reach representatives of national parties that gain large shares of the vote but do not get national representation because of the voting system, such as – in the case of the United Kingdom – the Green Party and UKIP. I also wanted to gauge whether there were any significant differences in outlook between national and European Parliament representatives, but in the event, as I set out in the book, I found that these were not as salient as might have been expected. The aim in qualitative research is to stop interviewing when you do not feel you are learning anything in each new interview, reaching "saturation point". In some cases, such as Denmark, I did think I reached saturation point. In other cases, such as the United States, where I did not think I reached enough "super" progressives, or France, where I could not reach significant numbers of Rassemblement National politicians, I was less satisfied. However, I have tried to be transparent on these points throughout.

The recruitment strategy worked as follows. For each country I drew up lists consisting of three categories: current "economic" ministers, such as top finance ministers, and in some cases tax or business ministers; their opposition party shadows; and key "economic committee" members, such as chairs. If I was rejected, I moved to secondary lists consisting of individuals who had held such posts in the last five years, and I broadened the committee chair category to committee membership. As anyone who has tried to interview politicians can attest, response rate patterns can seem random at times. Some high-profile former ministers agreed immediately on receipt of the first email, yet other less high-profile economic committee members had to be repeatedly pursued and still ended up refusing.

One non-country specific point to note is that there was, overall, a low response rate. We received four rejections or non-answers for every one acceptance. Three factors may explain the low response rate. First, there was the pandemic, which increased workloads and which it also took a while for support staff to adjust to. Second, there was the recent increase over the past decades in research requests, sometimes from students, which many interviewees alluded to. One retired MEP, who was totally engaged in the subject of our interview, said she would have instructed her assistant to reject my request out of hand if it had arrived while she was still in post. Third, the fact that we were inviting politicians to discuss their "economic ideas" anonymously rather than their importance, such as would have been the case if we had been researching a specific policy initiative with which they might have been identified and keen to get their account across for reputational reasons, may have depressed the response rate.

National differences in response rates, as well as institutional factors, led to variations in the nature of the country samples. The first area of difference related to proportions of current and non-current politicians. In the United States I could not, despite considerable effort, reach current politicians at all, because I did not have pre-existing contacts there and they were so heavily guarded by gatekeepers. However, I recommend interviewing former politicians. The accounts of the recently retired, including many former ministers, were as informative as the interviews with the current politicians; their memories were still fresh but they felt freer to speak. Nearly all the "former" politicians interviewed had retired or lost their seats within the preceding five years – in the US case, many in 2020.

Second, in terms of proportions of ministers in national samples, for institutional reasons, I interviewed only two former US ministers, because they tend not to be elected politicians (although it happened that one had been both). In Germany, I reached many opposition spokespeople but was not able to reach any who had previously served as ministers. In France, the UK and Denmark, politicians who had held ministerial status were much more forthcoming. Table A1 gives an overview of key characteristics of interviewees, such as gender, age, current or retired status, degree of "front bench" responsibility and amount of formal economics education.

The recruitment of advisers was less systematic than it was for politicians. In some cases when the politician refused, I asked his or her key economic adviser to conduct the interview instead. This was particularly useful in the American case, and most of those advisers serve current politicians. In other cases, where we could not get politicians from particular parties to agree, I targeted advisers. Table A2 gives an overview of adviser interviewee characteristics. (Tables A3 to A7 provide individual country details.)

The characteristics of our interviewees indicate that we were successful in our primary aim of eliciting input across the political spectrum, with the exception of the far right. Overall, our sample is strongly male-dominated, although women are generally under-represented in economics portfolios in Europe (Goddard 2019). The interviewees are also mainly over 50, with the exception of Denmark. Again, this partly affects the age profile of politicians. In the book I do occasionally highlight where age seems relevant. Finally, note the disproportionately high proportion of interviewees with some formal economics education. It seems likely that having an economics education leads politicians to choose economic committees and portfolios and also to be interested in our research project. Therefore, in this respect I must emphasize, again, that this book reflects the views of politicians who are among the most interested in economic ideas. This makes it even more significant that they are so dismissive of economists.

Table A1 Characteristics of politician interviewees by country

Country (number of politicians interviewed)	Currently elected	More than two modules university education*	National parliament rather than European	Male	Above 50	Leadership role**
Denmark (14)	50%	29%	71%	71%	50%	64%
France (19)	42%	53%	79%	68%	79%	42%
Germany (17)	29%	59%	65%	89%	94%	53%
UK (21)	33%	33%	76%	76%	86%	71%
United States (14)	0%	14%	100%	79%	93%	14%

Notes: * They had studied more than two modules of economics at university level.
** Either ministerial role or opposition spokesperson; does not include committee chairs.

Table A2 Characteristics of adviser interviewees by country

Country (number of advisers interviewed)	Serving currently elected politician	More than two modules university education*	National parliament rather than European	Male	Above 50	Leadership role**
Denmark 3 (far left, far right, centre)	100%	33%	66%	100%	33%	66%
France 1 (far left)	100%	0%	100%	100%	100%	0%
Germany 2 (right, Green)	100%	50%	0%	100%	0%	50%
UK 3 (one left, two far left)	0%	100%	100%	100%	66%	100%
United States 5 (two Democrat, 2 Republican, one non-partisan)	60%	40%	100%	60%	40%	80%

Notes: * They had studied more than two modules of economics at university level.
**Either ministerial role or opposition spokesperson; does not include committee chairs.

Table A3 French politicians

Party	Currently elected	Extent formal economic education	Parliament	Gender	Extent leadership role	Age
Left	Not current	School or two university modules	European	Female	Opposition spokesperson	61+
Right	Not current	School or two university modules	European	Female	No leadership position	61+
Left	Not current	School or two university modules	National	Male	Ministerial	61+
Right	Not current	More than two university modules	National	Male	Ministerial	61+

Table A3 (cont.)

Party	Currently elected	Extent formal economic education	Parliament	Gender	Extent leadership role	Age
Left	Not current	School or two university modules	National	Male	Ministerial	61+
Right	Not current	School or two university modules	National	Male	Ministerial	51–60
Right	Not current	More than two university modules	National	Male	No leadership position	51–60
Left	Current	School or two university modules	National	Male	No leadership position	51–60
Right	Current	More than two university modules	National	Male	Ministerial	61+
Right	Not current	School or two university modules	National	Male	No leadership position	61+
Right	Current	More than two university modules	National	Female	Ministerial	51–60
Far left	Current	Economist politician	European	Female	No leadership position	41–50
Left	Not current	Economist politician	National	Female	No leadership position	41–50
Centre	Current	More than two university modules	National	Male	No leadership position	51–60
Centre	Current	More than two university modules	National	Male	No leadership position	31–40
Far left	Current	More than two university modules	National	Male	Opposition spokesperson	61+
Centre	Current	School or two university modules	National	Female	No leadership position	21–30
Far right	Not current	Economist politician	European	Male	No leadership position	51–60
Right	Not current	School or two university modules	National	Male	No leadership position	51–60

Table A4 Danish politicians

Party	Currently elected	Extent formal economic education	Parliament	Gender	Extent leadership role	Age
Left	Current	School or two university modules	European	Female	No leadership position	51–60
Centre	Current	School or two university modules	National	Male	Ministerial	41–50
Far left	Current	School or two university modules	European	Male	No leadership position	31–40
Left	Not current	School or two university modules	National	Male	Ministerial	41–50
Left	Not current	Economist politician	National	Male	Ministerial	41–50
Left	Not current	Economist politician	National	Male	Ministerial	61+
Far left	Not current	School or two university modules	European	Female	No leadership position	31–40
Left	Current	None	National	Male	No leadership position	61+
Right	Not current	School or two university modules	National	Female	Ministerial	41–50
Centre	Not current	Economist politician	European	Female	No leadership position	61+
Far left	Current	Economist politician	National	Male	Opposition spokesperson	61+
Right	Not current	School or two university modules	National	Male	Ministerial	61+
Right	Current	More than two university modules	National	Male	Opposition spokesperson	51–60
Far right	Current	School or two university modules	National	Male	Opposition spokesperson	41–50

Table A5 German politicians

Party	Currently elected	Extent formal economic education	Parliament	Gender	Extent leadership role	Age
Right	Not current	More than two university modules	National	Male	No leadership position	61+
Far right	Current	School or two university modules	National	Male	Opposition spokesperson	61+
Left	Not current	Economist politician	National	Male	No leadership position	51–60
Green	Current	Economist politician	National	Female	Opposition spokesperson	51–60
Right	Not current	School or two university modules	National	Male	No leadership position	51–60
Far left	Not current	Economist politician	National	Male	Opposition spokesperson	61+
Left	Not current	School or two university modules	European	Male	No leadership position	51–60
Right	Not current	More than two university modules	European	Male	No leadership position	51–60
Left	Current	None	National	Male	Opposition spokesperson	61+
Right	Not current	None	European	Male	No leadership position	61+
Centre	Not current	Economist politician	European	Male	No leadership position	61+
Far Left	Current	More than two university modules	National	Male	Opposition spokesperson	61+
Green	Not current	School or two university modules	National	Male	Opposition spokesperson	61+
Far right	Not current	More than two university modules	European	Male	Opposition spokesperson	61+
Right	Not current	School or two university modules	National	Male	No leadership position	61+
Far right	Not current	Economist politician	European	Male	Opposition spokesperson	61+
Left	Current	Economist politician	National	Female	Opposition spokesperson	41–50

Table A6 UK politicians

Party	Currently elected	Extent formal economic education	Parliament	Gender	Extent leadership role	Age
Centre	Not current	Economist politician	National	Male	Ministerial	61+
Centre	Not current	None	National	Male	No leadership position	51–60
Left	Not current	School or two university modules	National	Male	Ministerial	61+
Green	Not current	Economist politician	European	Female	Opposition spokesperson	51–60
Right	Current	School or two university modules	National	Male	Ministerial	61+
Right	Not current	School or two university modules	National	Female	Ministerial	61+
Right	Not current	More than two university modules	National	Male	Ministerial	61+
Centre	Not current	None	European	Male	Opposition spokesperson	61+
Green	Not current	None	European	Female	Opposition spokesperson	61+
Left	Not current	None	European	Male	No leadership position	61+
Left	Not current	More than two university modules	National	Male	No leadership position	61+
Right	Current	More than two university modules	National	Male	No leadership position	51–60
Left	Current	None	National	Female	No leadership position	51–60
Far right	Not current	School or two university modules	European	Male	Opposition spokesperson	31–40
Far right	Current	More than two university modules	National	Male	Opposition spokesperson	51–60
Right	Not current	School or two university modules	National	Male	Ministerial	41–50
Right	Not current	School or two university modules	National	Male	Ministerial	51–60
Far right	Current	School or two university modules	National	Female	Ministerial	61+
Far right	Current	School or two university modules	National	Male	Opposition spokesperson	51–60
Right	Not current	More than two university modules	National	Male	Ministerial	51–60
Right	Current	School or two university modules	National	Male	No leadership position	31–40

Table A7 US politicians

Party	Currently elected	Extent formal economic education	Parliament	Gender	Extent leadership role	Age
Republican	Not current	Economist politician	National	Male	Ministerial	51–60
Republican	Not current	School or two university modules	National	Male	No leadership position	61+
Democrat	Not current	Economist politician	National	Male	No leadership position	61+
Republican	Not current	School or two university modules	National	Male	No leadership position	51–60
Republican	Not current	School or two university modules	National	Male	No leadership position	61+
Republican	Not current	School or two university modules	National	Male	No leadership position	51–60
Democrat	Not current	None	National	Male	No leadership position	61+
Democrat	Not current	School or two university modules	National	Female	No leadership position	61+
Democrat	Not current	School or two university modules	National	Female	No leadership position	61+
Republican	Not current	School or two university modules	National	Male	No leadership position	41–50
Republican	Not current	None	National	Male	No leadership position	61+
Republican	Not current	School or two university modules	National	Male	No leadership position	61+
Democrat	Not current	School or two university modules	National	Male	No leadership position	61+
Democrat	Not current	School or two university modules	National	Female	Ministerial	61+

References

Anthony, A. 2021. "Everything you wanted to know about the culture wars but were afraid to ask". *The Guardian*, 13 June. Available at: www.theguardian.com/world/2021/jun/13/everything-you-wanted-to-know-about-the-culture-wars-but-were-afraid-to-ask.

Berman, S. 2006. *The Primacy of Politics: Social Democracy and the Making of Europe's Twentieth Century*. Cambridge: Cambridge University Press.

Bertsou, E. 2020. "Conclusion: technocracy and democracy – friends or foes?". In *The Technocratic Challenge to Democracy*, E. Bertsou & D. Caramani (eds), 247–69. Abingdon: Routledge.

Bertsou, E. & D. Caramani (eds) 2020. *The Technocratic Challenge to Democracy*. Abingdon: Routledge.

Bevir, M. & R. Rhodes 2003. *Interpreting British Governance*. Abingdon: Routledge.

Baccaro, L. & J. Pontusson 2016. "Rethinking comparative political economy: the growth model perspective". *Politics & Society* 44 (2): 175–207.

Blumer, H. 1954. "What is wrong with social theory?" *American Sociological Review* 19 (1): 3–10.

Bonica, A. 2020. "Why are there so many lawyers in Congress?" *Legislative Studies Quarterly* 45 (2): 253–89.

Braun, V. & V. Clarke 2006. "Using thematic analysis in psychology". *Qualitative Research in Psychology* 3 (2): 77–101.

Braun, V. & V. Clarke 2013. *Thematic Analysis: A Practical Guide*. London: SAGE Publications.

Brownstein, R. 2021. "Bidenomics really is something new". *The Atlantic*, 6 May. Available at: www.theatlantic.com/politics/archive/2021/05/biden-economy-inflation-yellen/618816.

Bruère, M.-H. & D. Gaxie 2018. "Non-partisan ministers under the French Fifth Republic 1959–2014". In *Technocratic Ministers and Political Leadership in European Democracies*, A. Costa Pinto, M. Cotta & P. Tavares de Almeida (eds), 29–52. London: Palgrave Macmillan.

Burnham, P. 2001. "New Labour and the politics of depoliticisation". *British Journal of Politics & International Relations* 3 (2): 127–49.

Butler, C., R. Campbell & J. Hudson 2021. "Political recruitment under pressure, again: MPs and candidates in the 2019 general election". In *The British General Election of 2019*, R. Ford *et al.* (eds), 387–420. London: Palgrave Macmillan.

Buttler, M. 2021. "Denmark edges closer to historic decision on green debt issuance". Bloomberg, 3 November. Available at: www.bloomberg.com/news/articles/2021-11-03/denmark-edges-closer-to-historic-decision-on-green-debt-issuance.

Campbell, J. & O. Pedersen 2014. *The National Origins of Policy Ideas: Knowledge Regimes in the United States, France, Germany, and Denmark*. Princeton, NJ: Princeton University Press.

Caplan, B. 2007. *The Myth of the Rational Voter: Why Democracies Choose Bad Policies*. Princeton, NJ: Princeton University Press.

Caramani, D. 2020. "Introduction: the technocratic challenge to democracy". In *The Technocratic Challenge to Democracy*, E. Bertsou & D. Caramani (eds), 1–25. Abingdon: Routledge.

Carstensen, M. & N. Röper 2019. "Invasion from within: ideas, power and the transmission of institutional logics between policy domains". *Comparative Political Studies* 52 (9): 1328–63.

Christensen, J. 2017. *The Power of Economists within the State*. Stanford, CA: Stanford University Press.

Clift, B. 2016. "French economic policy: theory development and the three 'I's". In *The Oxford Handbook of French Politics*, R. Elgie, E. Grossman & A. Mazur (eds), 509–34. Oxford: Oxford University Press.

Coyle, D. 2021. *Cogs and Monsters: What Economics Is, and What It Should Be*. Princeton, NJ: Princeton University Press.

Cramer, K. 2016. *The Politics of Resentment: Rural Consciousness in Wisconsin and the Rise of Scott Walker*. Chicago, IL: University of Chicago Press.

Dahl, R. 1971. *Polyarchy: Participation and Opposition*. New Haven, CT: Yale University Press.

Daigneault, P. 2014. "Reassessing the concept of policy paradigm: aligning ontology and methodology in policy studies". *Journal of European Public Policy* 21 (3): 453–69.

De Gruyter, C. 2021. "Olaf Scholz's quiet revolution in German economics". Foreign Policy, 8 October. Available at: https://foreignpolicy.com/2021/10/08/olaf-scholzs-quiet-revolution-in-german-economics.

Disch, L. 2011. "Toward a mobilization conception of democratic representation". *American Political Science Review* 105 (1): 100–14.

Dunlop, C. & C. Radaelli 2020. "Technocracy and the policy process". In *The Technocratic Challenge to Democracy*, E. Bertsou & D. Caramani (eds), 183–96. Abingdon: Routledge.

Dyson, K. 2017. "Ordoliberalism as tradition and as ideology". In *Ordoliberalism, Law and the Rule of Economics*, J. Hien & C. Joerges (eds), 87–99. Oxford: Hart Publishing.

Erikson, R., M. MacKuen & J. Stimson 2002. *The Macro Polity*. Cambridge: Cambridge University Press.

Esaiasson, P. & C. Wlezien 2017. "Advances in the study of democratic responsiveness: an introduction". *Comparative Political Studies* 50 (6): 699–710.

Fawcett, E. 2020. *Conservatism: The Fight for a Tradition*. Princeton, NJ: Princeton University Press.

Fawcett, P. et al. 2017. *Anti-Politics, Depoliticization, and Governance*. Oxford: Oxford University Press.

Feld, L., E. Köhler & D. Nientiedt 2021. "The German anti-Keynes? On Walter Eucken's macroeconomics". *Journal of the History of Economic Thought* 43 (4): 548–63.

Fenno, R. 1966. *The Power of the Purse: Appropriations Politics in Congress*. Boston: Little, Brown.

Fenno, R. 1973. *Congressmen in Committees*. Boston, MA: Little, Brown.

Fiorino, D. 2018. *Can Democracy Handle Climate Change?* Cambridge: Polity Press.

Fourcade, M. 2009. *Economists and Societies: Discipline and Profession in the United States, Britain, and France, 1890s to 1990s*. Princeton, NJ: Princeton University Press.

Fourcade, M. 2018. "Economics the view from below". *Swiss Journal of Economics and Statistics* 154 (1): 1–19.

Galbraith, J. 2021. "The death of neoliberalism is greatly exaggerated". Foreign Policy, 4 June. Available at: https://foreignpolicy.com/2021/04/06/death-neoliberalism-larry-summ ers-biden-pandemic.

Gamble, A. 2017. "After Brexit: the past and future of the Anglo-liberal model". In *Diverging Capitalisms: Britain, the City of London and Europe*, C. Hay & D. Bailey (eds), 17–42. London: Palgrave Macmillan.

Georgescu-Roegen, N. 1971. *The Entropy Law and the Economic Process*. Cambridge, MA: Harvard University Press.

Goddard, D. 2019. "Entering the men's domain? Gender and portfolio allocation in European governments". *European Journal of Political Research* 58 (2): 631–55.

Hall, P. 1993. "Policy paradigms, social learning and the state: the case of economic policy-making in Britain". *Comparative Politics* 25 (3): 275–96.

Hall, P. 2006. "Introduction: the politics of social change in France". In *Changing France: The Politics that Markets Make*, P. Culpepper, P. Hall & B. Palier (eds), 1–25. Basingstoke: Palgrave.

Hall, P. 2018. "Varieties of capitalism in light of the euro crisis". *Journal of European Public Policy* 25 (1): 7–30.

Hall, P. & D. Soskice 2001. *Varieties of Capitalism: The Institutional Foundations of Comparative Advantage*. Oxford: Oxford University Press.

Hardin, G. 1968. "The tragedy of the commons". *Science* 162 (3859): 1243–8.

Harvey, W. 2011. "Strategies for conducting elite interviews". *Qualitative Research* 11 (4): 431–41.

Hayward, J. 1986. *The State and the Market Economy: Industrial Patriotism and Economic Intervention in France*. London: Wheatsheaf.

Hirschman, D. & E. Berman 2014. "Do economists make policies? On the political effects of economics". *Socio-Economic Review* 12 (4): 779–811.

Ilonszki, G. & S. Laurentiu 2018. "Variations in the expert ministerial framework in Hungary and Romania: personal and institutional explanations". In *Technocratic Ministers and Political Leadership in European Democracies*, A. Costa Pinto, M. Cotta & P. Tavares de Almeida (eds), 203–34. London: Palgrave Macmillan.

Jeffrey, A. 2018. "Limited epistocracy and political inclusion". *Episteme* 15 (4): 412–32.

Kemmerling, A. 2017. "Left without choice? Economic ideas, frames and the party politics of value-added taxation". *Socio-Economic Review* 15 (4): 777–96.

Kramer, C. 2017. "Vital stats: the growing influence of businesspeople in Congress". Brookings, 17 February. Available at: www.brookings.edu/blog/fixgov/2017/02/17/vital-stats-businesspeople-in-congress.

Kuzemko, C. 2014. "Politicising UK energy: what 'speaking energy security' can do". *Policy and Politics* 42 (2): 259–74.

Lavoie, M. 2006. "Do heterodox theories have anything in common? A post-Keynesian point of view". *European Journal of Economics and Economic Policies: Intervention* 3 (1): 87–112.

Lazear, E. 2000. "Economic imperialism". *Quarterly Journal of Economics* 115 (1): 99–146.

Loriaux, M. 1999. "The French developmental state as myth and moral ambition". In *The Developmental State*, M. Woo-Cummings (ed.), 235–75. Ithaca, NY: Cornell University Press.

Lovelock, J. 2009. *The Vanishing Face of Gaia: A Final Warning*. London: Allen Lane.

McCarty, N. 2019. *Polarization: What Everyone Needs to Know*. Oxford: Oxford University Press.

Machin, A. & G. Smith 2014. "Ends, means, beginnings: environmental technocracy, ecological deliberation or embodied disagreement?". *Ethical Perspectives* 21 (1): 47–72.

Mair, P. 2014. "Representative versus responsible government". In *On Parties, Party Systems and Democracy*, P. Mair (ed.), 581–96. Colchester: ECPR Press.

Majone, G. 1998. "Europe's democratic deficit: the question of standards". *European Law Journal* 4 (1): 5–28.

Mansbridge, J. 2003. "Rethinking representation". *American Political Science Review* 97 (4): 515–28.

Manwaring, R. & J. Holloway 2022. "A new wave of social democracy? Policy change across the Social Democratic Party family, 1970s–2010s". *Government and Opposition* 57 (1): 171–91.

Mason, L. 2018. *Uncivil Agreement: How Politics Became Our Identity*. Chicago, IL: University of Chicago Press.

Moravcsik, A. 2002. "Reassessing legitimacy in the European Union". *Journal of Common Market Studies* 40 (4): 603–24.

Mudde, C. & C. Kaltwasser 2017. *Populism: A Very Short Introduction*. Oxford: Oxford University Press.

Mudge, S. 2011. "What's left of leftism? Neoliberal politics in Western party systems, 1945–2004". *Social Science History* 35 (3): 337–80.

Mudge, S. 2018. *Leftism Reinvented: Western Parties from Socialism to Neoliberalism*. Cambridge, MA: Harvard University Press.

Newman, N. 2020. *Reuters Institute Digital News Report 2020*. Oxford: Reuters Institute for the Study of Journalism.

Pew Research Center 2019. "Public trust in government: 1958–2019". 11 November. Available at: www.pewresearch.org/politics/2019/04/11/public-trust-in-government-1958-2019.

Radaelli, C. 1999. *Technocracy in the European Union*. New York: Routledge.

Raworth, K. 2017. "Seven ways to think like a 21st century economist". OpenDemocracy, 5 April. Available at: www.opendemocracy.net/en/transformation/seven-ways-to-think-like-21st-century-economist.

Reay, M. 2012. "The flexible unity of economics". *American Journal of Sociology* 118 (1): 45–87.

Sánchez-Cuenca, I. 2020. "Neoliberal technocracy: the challenge to democratic self-government". In *The Technocratic Challenge to Democracy*, E. Bertsou & D. Caramani (eds), 44–60. Abingdon: Routledge.

Scott, J. 2021. "'There is no alternative'? The role of depoliticisation in the emergence of populism". *Politics*. DOI: 10.1177/0263395721990279.

Sedikides, C. & A. Gregg 2008. "Self-enhancement: food for thought". *Perspectives on Psychological Science* 3 (2): 102–16.

Semenova, E. 2018. "Recruitment and careers of ministers in Central Eastern Europe and Baltic countries". In *Technocratic Ministers and Political Leadership in European Democracies*, A. Costa Pinto, M. Cotta & P. Tavares de Almeida (eds), 173–202. London: Palgrave Macmillan.

Shearman, D. & J. Smith 2007. *The Climate Challenge and the Failure of Democracy*. Westport, CT: Praeger.

Sorley, W. 1926. *Tradition: The Herbert Spencer Lecture*. Oxford: Clarendon Press.

Stahl, R. 2022. "Neoliberalism with Scandinavian characteristics: the slow formation of neo-liberal common sense in Denmark". *Capital & Class* 46 (1): 95–114.

Stanley, B. 2008. "The thin ideology of populism". *Journal of Political Ideologies* 13 (1): 95–110.

Steffek, J. 2021. "Learning to love the technocrats again: why the world needs expertise now more than ever". London School of Economics and Political Science, 13 October. Available at: https://blogs.lse.ac.uk/europpblog/2021/10/13/learning-to-love-the-techno crats-again-why-the-world-needs-expertise-and-international-organisations-now-more-than-ever.

Sunak, R. 2021. "COP26 Finance Day speech". Gov.UK, 3 November. Available at: www.gov. uk/government/speeches/cop26-finance-day-speech.

Tomlinson, J. 2007. "Tale of a death exaggerated: how Keynesian policies survived the 1970s". *Contemporary British History* 21 (4): 429–48.

Tomlinson, J. 2017. *Managing the Economy, Managing the People: Narratives of Economic Life in Britain from Beveridge to Brexit*. Oxford: Oxford University Press.

van 't Klooster, J. 2021. "Technocratic Keynesianism: a paradigm shift without legislative change". *New Political Economy*. DOI: 10.1080/13563467.2021.2013791.

Walstad, W. & K. Rebeck 2002. "Assessing the economic knowledge and economic opinions of adults". *Quarterly Review of Economics and Finance* 42 (5): 921–35.

White, J. 2020. "COVID-19 crisis management blurs the boundary between politics and technocracy". London School of Economics and Political Science, 1 May. Available at: https://blogs.lse.ac.uk/covid19/2020/05/01/covid-19-crisis-management-blurs-the-boundary-between-politics-and-technocracy.

World Bank 2020. *Doing Business 2020: Comparing Business Regulation in 190 Economies*. Washington, DC: World Bank.

Index